LIFE IN
GEORGIAN LANCASTER

Watercolour drawing by
Gideon Yates of
Lancaster from the
Ridge, 1811.

Lancaster City Museums

Life in
Georgian Lancaster

ANDREW WHITE

Carnegie Publishing, 2004

First published in 2004 by
Carnegie Publishing Ltd
Carnegie House
Chatsworth Road, Lancaster LA1 4SL
www.carnegiepublishing.com

Copyright © Andrew White, 2004

ISBN 1-85936-102-1

All rights reserved

British Library Cataloguing-in-Publication data
A catalogue record for this book is available from the British Library

Designed, typeset and originated by Carnegie Publishing
Printed and bound in the UK by Cromwell Press, Trowbridge

Contents

Acknowledgements

This book began with an exhibition at Lancaster City Museum on the same subject. I naively thought that the exhibition labels would become the basis of a book, but in fact the book has grown and grown, and changed in character.

I would like to thank various people and institutions for their help in preparing this book. First of all I thank my former colleagues at Lancaster City Museums, especially Susan Ashworth, Dr. Nigel Dalziel, Ivan Frontani and Paul Thompson. The reference staff at Lancaster Central Library, particularly Jenny Loveridge, helped with illustrations and documents. The Manchester Central Library and Society of Antiquaries Library, London, produced many rare volumes. Martin Widden and Peter Hearne were generous in letting me see their Deeds (part of a huge project which involved many other lenders). At the Lancashire Record Office Andrew Thynne was most helpful in producing relevant Probate Inventories. Cumbria Record Office and Liverpool Libraries allowed me to use items in the Soulby collection and Binns Collection respectively.

front cover Lancaster from Cable St, a painting by Julius Caesar Ibbetson. (*Lancaster City Museums*)

back cover Lancaster Castle, Court House, and Church, 1833, engraved by T. Higham after T. Allom.

back cover (inset) Portrait by the cartoonist John Nixon of Dr William Barrow, who died after falling out of his upper window while trying to read the time by the Town Hall clock in 1791. (*Lancaster City Museums*)

Introduction

The Georgian period ran from the accession of George I in 1715 to the death of George IV in 1830. It covered a long period of time and included many changes in the way people lived and thought. It saw rebellion (the 1715 and 1745 Jacobite Risings), war (particularly the Seven Years War with France in 1756–63, the American colonies and their French allies from 1776 onwards, and France again, ending at Waterloo in 1815), the growth of the British Empire and the birth of the Industrial Revolution. By the end of this period Britain had become the richest and most powerful nation in the world.

We associate the Georgian period with elegance, fine furniture, confidence, prosperity and humanity. It also had its dark side – slavery; a savage penal code which included the death penalty for quite minor offences; social inequality; unfair political representation; and appalling conditions in early mines and factories made the lot of many thousands of people anything but secure and elegant. But there were also many redeeming features. The country was thinly populated; the poor were not as poor or the rich as rich as they were to become later in the nineteenth century; the cities were less crowded and disease-ridden; society was less rigid. Many foreigners marvelled at the freedom and confidence of ordinary Britons, at the size and splendour of London, and at the prosperity of town and countryside.

It would be a mistake to think of this as a 'Golden Age' for everyone. It was a matter of perspective, and you would not have thought this if you were a slave, one of the rural poor, in almost perpetual hunger, or someone about to be executed for the theft of a loaf of bread or operated upon without anaesthetic. The Georgian period has, however, left us a vast legacy of fine buildings, town planning, furniture, ceramics, art and literature. It has also left a sense of a period more akin to our own than the intervening stuffy and pious Victorian period. It was an age filled with humanity, common sense and clear-sightedness.

CHAPTER ONE

The Town

New beginnings

Lancaster began the eighteenth century as a small market town, enlivened twice a year by the Assizes held at the Castle. Much of its business was in sheep and cattle, butter and cheese. Small specialist shops, lawyers and land agents served the surrounding rural area. Country people and farmers called in on market days to buy nails, candles or cloth, make wills, transfer property and transact business in the many inns. At the Assizes, held in spring and autumn, all the criminal and civil actions of the whole county of Lancashire were tried in the town. The lawyers and barristers and neighbouring gentry came to town and entertained each other at social events.

Growth came with prosperity from overseas trade. Accurate assessments of population before the national census began in 1801 are hard to come by. We have to extrapolate figures from other information. Assuming an average of 5–6 people per house we can put a figure of 1,600–1,900 to the population of Lancaster in 1684, right at the beginning of Lancaster's prosperity.[1] An estimate of 1750, of dubious quality, put the population at 6,500, while a survey by the parish clerk in 1784 suggested that there were then 8,584 people in the town, excluding seamen.[2] From 1801 we are on more secure ground; in that year the numbers were 9,030 (again excluding seamen), in 1811 9,247, in 1821 10,144 and in 1831 12,167.[3] The rise was by no means meteoric and contrasts markedly with that of many other Lancashire towns. Nonetheless a town of about 10,000 people in the Georgian period was a significant place, and in Lancaster's case the absence of a substantial textile industry before about 1820 avoided the polarisation between extreme wealth and poverty visible in many Lancashire towns. It was also the county town, which, as we shall see, gave it a number of differences and advantages.

Overseas trade began in a small way. At the end of the seventeenth century a few small tradesmen such as the ironmonger William Stout started to take an interest in shipping goods to the American colonies and to the West Indies. Many of these people were Quakers – members of the Society of Friends – who were barred by their religious beliefs from taking part in the professions, such as the law or medicine, or offices of state. They formed a small and close-knit community, in touch with fellow Quakers in other ports and even in America – Pennsylvania had been first colonised by Quakers. The small ventures became larger and more lucrative. Soon, many who had been content to be tradesmen began to call themselves merchants. Income derived from overseas trade began to be invested in new houses and the whole townscape began to change, with the rebuilding of older and unfashionable houses in existing streets and then the opening up of new streets and even whole new developments.[4]

The pace of change grew as the century wore on. The 1780s and 1790s in particular saw a frenzy of building, with a new bridge over the river Lune (now known as Skerton Bridge), a new aqueduct to carry the Lancaster Canal, a new Town Hall, a new Theatre and an elegant development in the Fryerage, site of the medieval Friary, which was called Dalton Square. The building boom was matched by a desire for new clothes, new events at which to show them off, new furniture, and new interior decoration, and by growing expectations of even greater things to come.

The key to much of the prosperity had been the Act of Parliament passed in 1749 concerned with the navigation of the river Lune.

The south-west corner of Dalton Square, showing the original painted street name which was revealed when the metal sign was moved. Dalton Square was deliberately set up as Lancaster's premier address, and succeeded to an extent, but the timing coincided with a lasting downturn in Lancaster's economy, which reduced the demand for large houses which were designed for entertaining.

right No 23 St George's Quay, an amazingly crooked house which settled during building work and still displays attempts to level it up. These buildings were constructed on river clay, rubbish and stones and often lack decent foundations.

left Portrait by the cartoonist John Nixon of Dr William Barrow, who died after falling out of his upper window while trying to read the time by the Town Hall clock in 1791. Barrow was one of the most active proponents of the scheme to develop Dalton Square and had leased all the lots on the north side in 1783, but by his death had not yet built upon them. His heir James subdivided the four large lots into twelve, and it was built up by 1798.

Lancaster City Museums

The subsequent building of a new quay just downstream of the old bridge in 1750, known as St George's Quay, was a direct consequence. This quay allowed ships to unload their cargoes in safety at most stages of the tide. Cargoes could then be carted to warehouses, some thirty of which lined the quay by 1780, for storage. There were also many other warehouses scattered about the town. A new Custom House was also built on the quay in 1764 to control the duties on the growing range of imports. Sugar, tobacco, rum, spices, mahogany and dyestuffs came in, while finished goods, including foodstuffs and furniture, went out. Many of the houses and warehouses can still be seen, while the Custom House is now Lancaster's Maritime Museum. St George's Quay itself is a very rare example of an almost unchanged eighteenth-century port, left behind by the developments in building and fireproofing which wrought such changes in the nineteenth century to London, Liverpool and Bristol, for instance.

Shipbuilding also took place on the river. Two shipyards of long standing were in operation from about 1740, although perhaps not continuously. One on the south bank, on Green Ayre, roughly where Sainsbury's store stands today, was run by the Brockbank family. Another on the north bank, near the end of the Old Bridge, passed through several hands, perhaps beginning under Thomas Wakefield and continuing under Smiths and Ashburners. William

right Tombstone of James Booth, the longest-serving Collector of Customs for the port of Lancaster, from at least 1779 to 1834. His portrait can be seen in Lancaster Maritime Museum.

A typical warehouse on St George's Quay. The central slots gave admission to long open timber-floored spaces behind, into which heavy goods were lifted by means of the derrick at the top. The small windows at either side lit counting-houses where clerks could record movement of stock.

right Lancaster from Cable St, a painting by Julius Caesar Ibbetson. On the right is Brockbank's shipyard with a large West-Indiaman on the stocks. The whole foreground formed part of the Green Ayre, originally an open space in the bend of the river where Lancastrians took their leisure. From the 1740s, however, it was being developed with streets and merchants' quays and warehouses.

Lancaster City Museums

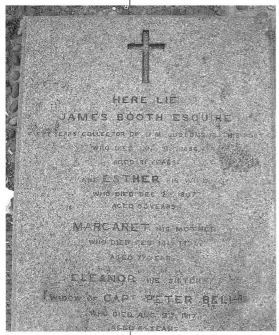

Stout was injured here by a runaway horse while watching a ship being fitted out for the West Indies in 1743.[5]

I left my house at eight a clock and walked over Lancaster Bridge, at the end of which some carpenters of my acquaintance were fitting out a ship intended for Jamaica, with whom I talked about two minutes upon the shore, out of the high way, and then turned to the way to go forward. And seeing a boy on horseback coming toward me at full speed, I stepped to the side, out of his way as I thought, but the horse came right upon me on his blind side full speed ...

War and Peace

A small paper pennant with PEACE in gilt letters, dating from the Peace of Amiens in 1801–2. This short break in hostilities was followed by another twelve years of war, but gave a much-needed breathing-space to Britain.

Lancaster City Museums

Twice in the eighteenth century, in 1715 and 1745, Lancaster had the experience of being in the path of a potentially hostile Jacobite army, bringing the realities of war very close to home. As it happened the Jacobites were generally well behaved and disciplined, and had no particular grudge against the townspeople, but Lancaster had experienced looting and burning by Scottish armies twice in the fourteenth century and could afford to take no chances, particularly on the Jacobite return from Derby in 1745, when tensions ran high.[6] One of the invaders, John Maclean, left a first-hand account.[7]

> ... we entered the Good and Large Town of Lancaster in Lancashire ... Lancaster is a seaport Town & has a very large Strand below it, and has a Castle & a handsome bridge. Monday the 25 all the Calvallry and infantry we had there were turned to a Parade at the Cross, and the Provost and Bailies were Called & the Provost Appeared in his velvet Gown and a Black rod with a Silver head. And upon the Cross they proclaimed the King and afterwards we marched ten miles that Day and quartered at Garstang ...

More distant wars formed the background to a large part of the Georgian period. In particular the Seven Years War, the War of American Independence and the wars with revolutionary and Napoleonic France brought home to mercantile and seafaring people in Lancaster the realities of loss and capture. Paying for wars with money or lives affected more or less the whole population and the number of items and services which were taxed grew and grew. By the end of the eighteenth century, the fervour of patriotism meant that a great many families had someone serving in the army or navy, or more probably in one of the many militia or yeomanry units which were raised to protect the country against invasion. Scarlet uniforms were a commonplace on the streets and subscriptions were raised to provide uniforms and food.

Militia were raised locally. Officers volunteered but in most cases the private soldiers were chosen by lot from each parish from a list of able-bodied men. The original lists still survive for the 1757 call-up of militia.[8] The process was repeated during the Napoleonic Wars at the end of the eighteenth and beginning of the nineteenth century. Those chosen by ballot could, and did, find someone else to take their place, by paying them, if they could afford to do so. Local militia paraded and exercised in their home town but in times of high tension, such as 1803–5, when invasion of Britain by the French seemed not only likely but inevitable, many were marched to the south coast to act as a garrison in the event of invasion. The militia men were traditionally billeted in public houses and a rare survival of evidence for this comes from the borough court records, where in 1813 the list of contents of Richard Hamer's inn includes a room called 'The Soldiers Barwick' [barracks]. It was evidently disused.[9]

Sailors were in constant risk at this time of being impressed into the Navy, although merchant shipping had a great need for manpower and was almost as risky. Passes could be obtained – at a cost – by skilled workmen which gave them immunity from being impressed. Such was the case with William Mackreth, one of John Brockbank's shipwrights (see illustation, left).

Shipping suffered from the depredations of French privateers and heavy losses were met by Lancaster merchants. For the crews, unless an exchange of prisoners was made, then a long spell as a prisoner-of-war in France could result. Ships without sufficient guns to protect themselves had to sail in convoy; but convoys meant that ships arrived together, causing a glut of commodities and lowering prices. Quaker merchants were not allowed to arm their ships; a few did, and were disowned by the Quaker community. This was due to the principle of pacificism to which the Quakers adhered. Armed merchantmen might obtain 'letters of marque', permitting them to act as privateers. Lancaster privateers

Certificate issued in 1780 by John Brockbank, shipbuilder, to protect William Mackreth, one of his journeymen shipwrights, from the attentions of the Press Gang. Because of the importance of the shipbuilding industry to the survival of Britain during the Napoleonic Wars, it was regarded as an exempt occupation. Merchant seamen were not so lucky, and could be snatched from their ship at the end of a long voyage without the chance evn to alert their families.

Lancaster Central Library

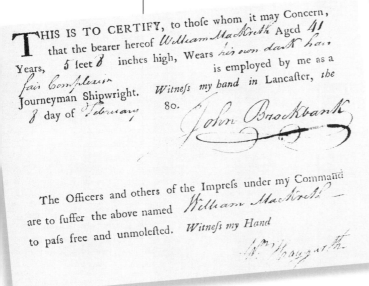

took French ships, too, and there were occasional rich prizes to be had. The Lancaster ship *Thetis* fought off a much larger French ship *Bonaparte* in an action off Barbados in 1804, protecting several smaller vessels in the process. Both sides of the story can be seen in the case of Captain Weeton, who, according to his daughter, was the toast of the town for his brave exploits during the American War of Independence, and was owed a great deal of prize-money by the Rawlinsons, his employers, when he was suddenly killed in an encounter with an American ship in about 1782, leaving his family destitute.[10]

> My father was for some time captain of a merchantman in the African slave trade, but the American war breaking out, he was next commissioned by the Rawlinsons of Lancaster (distant relations of my mother's) to command a vessel carrying a Letter of Marque. In this vessel he sailed, and in the course of his voyage took many prizes ... For some months glowing accounts came of my father's valour and success ... when one evening the Jamaica packet arrived, but – no letter for her [her mother]. She immediately set out for Mr. James Hinde's, where she was intimate, who had a son abroad, and found them reading a letter from him giving an account of my father's death ...
>
> Her sufferings were very great; for she not only lost a kind husband, but was defrauded out of the whole of his prize money and other property gained by his voyages, by the Rawlinsons ...

right Monument in Lancaster Priory church to Rev. William White, who unfortunately took advantage of the Peace of Amiens in 1802 to travel in France, only to be interned at the resumption of hostilities; he died later at Verdun.

In the north-west corner of the Priory churchyard stands this classical monument topped by an urn, commemorating members of the Rawlinson family and their relations by marriage. The Rawlinsons became the principal merchant dynasty in the town, with fingers in almost every pie. One of their sea-captains, William Lindow, married Abigail Rawlinson and they lived in Queen Square. Both are buried here.

Loss and disruption were the more usual lot of Lancaster shipping, however, than rich prizes.

Even civilians could find trouble. Rev. William White, vicar of Lancaster in succession to Dr. Oliver Marton, whose brother-in-law he was, had the misfortune to be travelling in France when the brief Treaty of Amiens (1801–2) came to an end. He was imprisoned and died in captivity at Verdun in 1806. His monument on the south wall of Lancaster Priory church tells the sad story.[11] Lancaster Castle was used as one of the many prisons for French POWs, a fact hitherto only suspected but now proved by the travel journal of Richard Holden, 1808.[12]

… the Castle worth seeing and the View from the Terrace & from the Church Yard charming – the Additions of the Law Courts in the Castle finely done in good gothic taste by Gandy the Architect – but the passages for the Suitors dangerously narrow – the prisoner into the bar through the Trap Door & conveyed out again the same way – Many French prisoners in the body of the Castle now.

Lancaster City Museums have two items which appear to have been made by French POWs, perhaps in Lancaster Castle. They are a fitted box, decorated with split-straw marquetry work, and a decorative games compendium containing playing cards and dominoes made of thin sheets of bone, traditionally from the meat ration. Such items were made by teams of prisoners, overseen by skilled straw-workers (France pioneered the technique) and ivory carvers such as those from Dieppe, where the trade had long been established.[13]

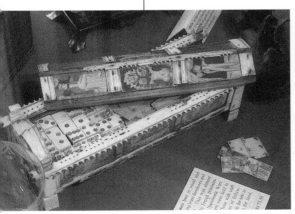

A games compendium decorated with cut and painted bone-work and containing thin bone dominoes and playing cards. This is typical of the work of French prisoners-of-war during the Napoleonic Wars, aimed at earning money from visitors to supplement the meagre rations. *Lancaster City Museums*

A fitted workbox decorated in coloured split-straw marquetry, also typical of French POW work. Skilled craftsmen among the prisoners would carry out the showiest bits while the less capable helped with the basic wooden structure, in a sort of assembly-line. *Lancaster City Museums*

War and Peace

Lancaster was doubly involved in the state of war which prevailed for much of the Georgian period. Firstly, it was on the main west-coast road and so lay on the route of the Jacobite armies in both 1715 and 1745, so tasting at first hand the occupation and petty looting which for most Englishmen was something which went on abroad. Secondly its commitment as a port to trade with the West Indies and the America colonies brought it into conflict with French privateers in the Seven Years War, the War of American Independence, the Napoleonic Wars and the American War of 1812, with consequent losses.

Lonsdale Regiment of Local Militia,
In the County of Lancaster.

THIS is to certify, that *John Newby* is enrolled a Private in the Lonsdale Regiment of Local Militia, in the County of Lancaster, and that he has joined the said Regiment, now assembled at Lancaster, for the purpose of Exercise during *14* Days next ensuing. GIVEN under my Hand at Lancaster, the *11th* Day of *May* 1812

John Bradshaw Lieut. Col. Comt.
Lonsdale Local Militia.

left Certificate of enrolment of John Newby into the Lonsdale Regiment of Local Militia, 1812. This body of 360 men was raised to meet the threat of invasion by the French in the Autumn of 1803, along with similar militias in towns and cities all over Britain. As a sort of Home Guard, the men were placed under arms and in training for two weeks each year, usually away from their home town. The certificate may have been a device to help members to avoid being pressed by the Royal Navy.

Lancaster Central Library

left Replica uniforms in evidence at one of Lancaster's Georgian Festivals. These featured accurate period costuming and behaviour and gave a very good impression of the age. For a great part of the Georgian period scarlet uniforms of both regular soldiery and the militias must have seemed omnipresent, given the almost perpetual state of conflict.

Many of the male adult population became involved, either as mariners or as soldiers, regulars or militia. The militia and the Navy had a habit of demanding the services of key personnel in the shipbuilding trade, so such men often obtained immunity, or paid for an alternative to serve. In the very real threat of invasion in 1803–5 many of the militia were moved down to the south coast.

Ships and men were lost to privateers, but there were gains also, including a number of rich prizes captured by Lancaster ships. French POWs, too, were held in Lancaster Castle, and brought a number of new skills with them including split straw work, which indirectly led to new fashions in women's hats, and employment for unmarried women!

The sound of fife and drum and the sight of redcoats – a frequent experience for Lancaster's Georgian citizens and replicated here at a Georgian Festival.

right List of subscribers to a fund for soldiers and sailors, set up in a time of national emergency in 1793–94. An open list encouraged well-off citizens to try to outdo each other in generosity, or at least to match the gifts of their social equals.

Lancaster Central Library

The Names of the Persons who have Subscribed as under,

FOR RAISING A SUM OF MONEY

To be applied in Purchasing Cloaths, or other neceſſary Articles

FOR THE

SEAMEN & SOLDIERS

Now employed in his MAJESTY's Service.

	£. s.			£. s. d.
...Tallon Eſq; Mayor	5 5		Mr. William Bryer	61 19
...Cawthorne Eſq; Recorder	5 5		Mr. Thomas Worſwick	1 1 0
Mr. Marton	5 5		Mr. B. Satterthwaite	1 1 0
...Gibſon Eſq;	3 3		John Lawſon Eſq;	1 1 0
...inſon Eſq;	2 2		James Hinde Eſq;	1 1 0
...tterthwaite Eſq;	2 2		Mr. William Thompſon	10 6
...h Eſq;	2 2		Mr. John Stout	10 6
...lurd Eſq;	2 2		Mrs. Lewthwaite	10 6
...llſon, Square	2 2		Mr. Robert Hinde	10 6
...lſon, Church-ſtreet	2 2		Miſs D. Robinſon	10 6
...Rigby Eſq;	1 1		Miſs E. Robinſon	10 6
...ones Eſq;	1 1		Rev. Mr. Widditt	10 6
...uckley Eſq;	1 1		Wm. Parke Eſq;	10 6
...rd Saart, Senior	1 1		Mr. Thomas Burrow	10 6
...s Eſq;	1 1		Mr. John Watkinſon	10 6
...Barrow, Senior	1 1		Mr. James Moore	10 6
...d Johnſon	1 1		Mr. William Stout	10 6
...ſon Eſq;	1 1		Mrs. Tindall	10 6
...y Charnley	1 1		Mr. Richard Walker	10 6
Rev. Mr. John Rigby	1 1		Mr. Thomas Shepherd	10 6
Mr. John Brockbank	1 1		Mr. James Weights	10 6
Mr. Edward Saart, Junior	1 1		Mr. James Parkinſon, Attorney	10 6
Mr. Thomas Brayſhaw	1 1		Mr. John Dowbiggin ditto	10 6
Mr. John Armongſtrong	1 1		Mr. George Poſtlethwaite	10 6
Mr. Robert Gillow	1 1		Doctor Campbell	10 6
Mr. Chriſtopher Butterfield	1 1		Mr. Wm. Feddon	10 6
Mr. Joſeph Barclay	1 1		Mr. Richard Atkinſon	10 6
Mr. Alexander Worſwick	1 1		Mr. James Tinning	10 6
Rev. Mr. Pedder	1 1		Mr. John Langſhaw	10 6
Mr. Thomas Clarkſon	1 1		Mr. Iſaac Hammond	5 0
Mr. William Fiſher	1 1		Mr. Chriſtopher Sherſon	5 0
Mr. Jackſon Maſon	1 1		Mr. William Coward	5 0
Mr. Chriſtopher Bradſhaw	1 1		Mr. A. Buſher	5 0
Mr. E. Saliſbury, Church-ſtreet	1 1		Mr. William Barr	5 0
Doctor Harris	1 1		Mr. Edward Batty	3 0
Doctor Wright	1 1		Mr. Stephen Wrathell	2 6
Thomas Hind Eſq;	1 1		Mr. Joſeph Weedon	2 6
Mr. John Higgin	1 1		Mr. William Marſhall	2 0
Doctor Baxendale	1 1			
£ 61 19			£ 80 12 6	

☞ The above Sum beſides the Corporation Subſcription of 20 Guineas hath been remitted to Mr. JOHN HERIOT Strand, London, to be by him applied for the Purpoſes abovementioned.

County Town Life

Since the Middle Ages Lancaster had been the county town of Lancashire, a fact that was very significant to the daily life of its inhabitants. Lancaster's position did not go unchallenged, and Lancaster people were very aware of what benefits the status brought to the town and what their loss would entail. Equally, other towns were aware of the economic and social advantages of being the county town, and viewed Lancaster's position with envy. Preston was larger, while Liverpool was almost metropolitan in character and, with the rather less-sophisticated Manchester, formed a huge concentration of population in the very southernmost part of the county. Although their growth was entirely post-medieval, the south Lancashire towns made the county very unbalanced and rendered the framework designed for the administration of what had been a poor and backward area in the Middle Ages seem very much out of date.

Today Lancaster seems very far north in the county to be its capital. But the shrunken county of today does not tell the whole story. Medieval and early-modern Lancashire included a vast tract of land to the north-west, including the Furness and Cartmel peninsulas, together with Coniston and the western side of Windermere. This area, the old 'Hundred of Lonsdale North of the Sands', was a land with no towns of any consequence until the nineteenth century, except for Ulverston. When young men from this area sought apprenticeship it was across the Bay to Lancaster that they looked.

By the eighteenth century both Liverpool and Manchester were beginning to leave behind their more northerly neighbours, but old habits and rules died hard. The old county town retained the Assizes and various other functions on which others looked greedily, as much because of the economic benefits as because of the inconvenience of getting there to transact their business.

The county as a unit of government had been insignificant in earlier days. County Councils did not come into being until 1889 and their manifold functions were still far in the future. However, some functions sat uneasily with the essentially local system of government, because they crossed traditional boundaries. Roads and bridges had long been an anomaly. It had been a bone of contention since Elizabethan times that those whose parish lay

The New Bridge (now Skerton Bridge) engraved by Landseer after Farington, 1791. This beautiful flat-decked bridge on five elliptical arches was designed by Thomas Harrison, its design based on the Roman bridge at Rimini. It struck a chord with the classical tastes of the age and was much painted, along with the equally classical Aqueduct Bridge which carries the Lancaster Canal over the river Lune.

Lancaster City Museums

along a main road had the misfortune to contribute to its maintenance and, indeed, to work on it free of charge when required. The users, in contrast, had no duties at all to contribute to its upkeep, until the rise of the turnpikes. Likewise bridges had become a burden rather than a benefit. From the late seventeenth century the county, through the court of Quarter Sessions (so called because it was adjourned to sit four times each year), had taken responsibility for the upkeep and rebuilding of many bridges, previously the responsibility of the Hundred. Therefore, the new Skerton Bridge was paid for by the county – fortunately so, as it cost £14,000 and might not have been built half as attractively or as sturdily had it not been so funded.

By the end of the eighteenth century a range of new or enhanced duties had landed on the counties, leading to the rebuilding of courts and prisons, such as Lancaster Castle, and the creation of Lunatic Asylums for each county.[14] Previous to this lunatics had been kept in appalling conditions in the Castle. In 1811 the borough presented five acres of land on the Moor to the county

authorities for the building of the new County Lunatic Asylum. It was not entirely altruistic in its gift. It sought to reaffirm county town status by these means, and to derail plans to build the asylum elsewhere. It was also argued that the building work could be done much more cheaply because the stone was available close by at the Moor quarries, while the visitation by magistrates, an essential part of its governance, could be conveniently combined with other legal business in the town.[15]

The presence of the Assizes gave the town a strong economic benefit, felt particularly by the inns and providers of stabling and other services. There was also a social benefit. The aristocracy and gentry tended to be drawn into town by the courts, for service on the Grand Jury or to transact their estate business. The establishment of horse-races on the Marsh and later at Syke Swamp on Lancaster Moor provided another focus for gatherings and the theatre and other cultural activities blossomed, especially during race-week in June and the spring and autumn Assizes. County towns were strengthening their position by the end of the eighteenth century, rather than weakening, despite the growth of other towns often outstripping their own in size or economic development.

The idea of a county identity was just beginning to emerge at about this time, especially in gentry circles. The county provided a focus for their loyalty and a relatively small social grouping within which to move. With or without

The County Lunatic Asylum, built by the county on a piece of Lancaster Moor given by the Corporation. The central block is the oldest part and dates from 1811–16. It represented a huge step forward in mental care. Previously 'lunatics' – a wide description for a whole range of conditions – had been confined in the Castle in exceedingly grim conditions. The new Asylum was given the appearance of a country house.

that other great group, the clergy, the gentry of the county made loyal addresses, raised money for charitable or political purposes, and challenged other counties at such pseudo-sporting events as cock-fighting. Lancaster was doubly fortunate in that it lay near the northern boundary of Lancashire. It thus appealed to gentry from Westmorland, who regarded it as a centre for specialised goods and services, in preference to Kendal, which was smaller, or Appleby, the county town of Westmorland, which was both smaller and less convenient.

Contrasts

Many merchants and their families found themselves enjoying lives of elegance and plenty, if not of ease. Their houses could be seen on the main streets, newly rebuilt and with all the trappings of comfort, including servants, stables and carriages.

Numbers 5–7 Queen St are a pair of large and elegant houses belonging to the 1770s. The eccentric Quaker Daniel Eccleston lived at Number 5 for a time. The ironwork outside is remarkably complete, and includes contemporary railings and standard for an oil lamp.

There were other people of humbler origin, particularly former farm workers from the country-side around, who – attracted by the prosperity of the town – came to Lancaster to try their fortunes. This was the beginning of a long flight from the land, brought about by a combination of the industrial revolution, a less dramatic agricultural revolution and higher expectations from life. To house these aspirants, landlords ran up rows of cheap cottages on former gardens behind the bigger houses on the main streets and rented them out. The town began to grow in on itself. Other poorer people rented rooms in shared older and unfashionable houses. It was quite usual for unmarried men to take a room in a larger house, perhaps having meals brought into them. William Stout did this on at least three occasions, the first in 1691 and the last in 1730.[16]

> John Bryer and I took the rest [of the house]. He had the kitchin part with the roomes over it entire to him selfe. I had the great parlor, seller under it and three bed rooms above, but the stairs to them was common with them who inhabited the street part ...
>
> In the first month this year [1730], I gave up housekeeping and lett my house to Mary and Lidia Dillworth [two wealthy Quaker spinsters]. And borded and lodged with them at the rate of 12 pounds a year, and continued with them, and they in the house, three years ...

Elderly widows might eke out a living by cooking and washing for such people.

In the Georgian period there was no particular rich area – or poor area – in Lancaster. Both rich and poor often lived side by side on the older streets such as Church Street. Castle Hill, however, was a favoured place for merchants to live and contained the houses of several of the Rawlinson family as well as Satterthwaites, Harrisons and others of the merchant elite. On the other hand few wealthy people could be found in Stonewell or Rosemary (known as 'Stinking') Lane, where life expectancy was short. Generally the higher one lived towards the Castle Hill the greater one's income and likelihood of living to old age, although the seepage of the graveyard on the hill above could foul wells and deliver mortal sickness even in this area.

A good deal of Lancaster's new-found wealth was based on the slave trade.

A sad story is associated with this memorial. Sybill Wilson was the daughter of Lt Col George Wilson and his wife Anne Sybill, herself the daughter of the wealthy Allan Harrison who lived at 20 Castle Park and had built a row of five houses nearby to fund his daughter's dowry. Wilson built Abbot Hall at Kendal in 1759, but after their daughter's death at the age of six the pair moved to York. It was her grandparents who encouraged them to have the little girl buried at Lancaster, near them.

It was highly specialised and some ships were not involved at all while others did nothing else. Slavery as a state did not exist in Great Britain itself, but it did in the British colonies, and the trade was legally carried out from a number of ports until it was eventually abolished in 1807. In the rest of the British Empire slave-owning continued until 1834 and it survived in the southern states of America until the Civil War of 1861–65.

Many people in Britain were fundamentally opposed to the very idea of slavery. Quakers, in particular, attacked it at every opportunity and men such as Clarkson and Wilberforce spent much of their lives fighting its evils. In the 1750s, however, Lancaster had the dubious honour of being the fourth most active port in the trade, and there were even several Quakers involved in the trade, despite their religious beliefs.

Slaving ships set off for West Africa loaded with trade goods, including beads, trinkets and firearms. These they exchanged for slaves at a number of recognised slave ports on the African coast, where traders brought them from inland. The black slaves, terrified, disorientated and separated from their loved ones, were tightly packed onto the small vessels and taken to America or the West Indies. Many died on the way from disease or the appalling conditions. Those who arrived alive could look forward to a life of extreme labour, cruelty and complete absence of human rights. In return for these slaves, ships brought back to Britain a range of high-value raw materials. This arrangement was known as the 'Triangular Trade' and relied on Lancaster merchants having reliable agents in the foreign ports. Because the slaves themselves did not come back to Britain the population as a whole did not see the evils of the trade and saw only the cash benefits. This does not make them any less guilty of collusion. Lancaster's involvement was fairly short-lived, as the slaving ships became larger and the trade became confined to a few large ports, namely

A plan of 1830, based upon one of 1816, accompanying deeds for property in Swan Court, off St Leonardgate. Typically there are a number of larger properties on the street frontage while a passage leads through to cottages for rent at the rear. The curious layout matches the original croft upon which these cottages were built. In the seventeenth century there was a tannery here with a bark-house, while the name goes back to the Swan with Two Necks, an inn recorded on the frontage in 1729.

Lancaster City Council Deeds

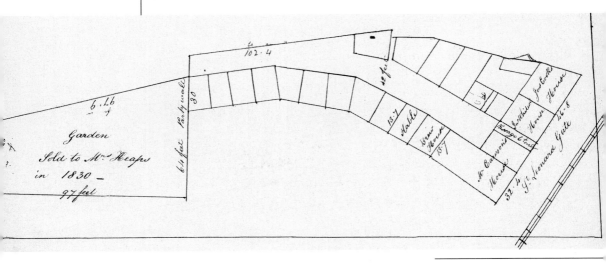

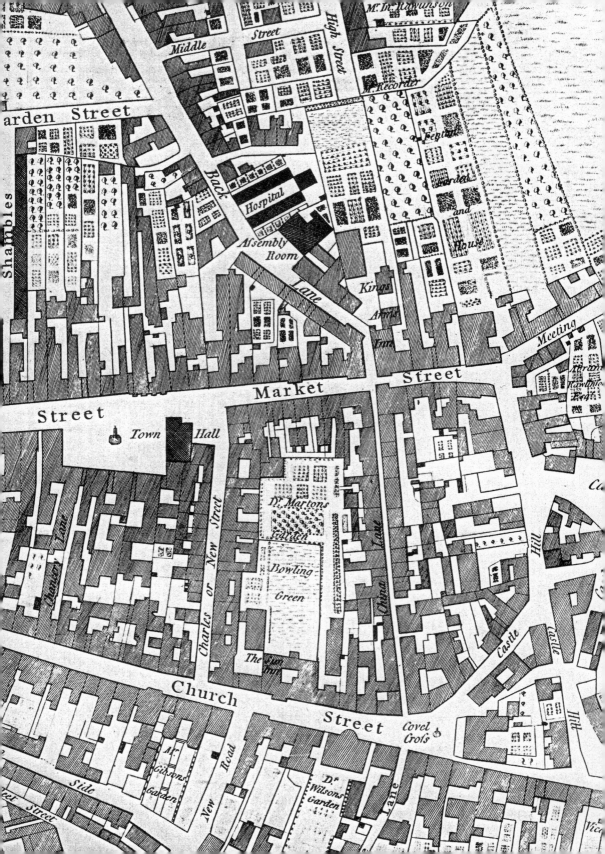

left Lancaster town centre from Mackreth's map of 1778 (with north to the bottom). The built-up area was still fairly small and despite the start of a building boom new develop-ments were as yet confined to New Street, St George's Quay, High Street and Queen Street. There were still many older buildings in the main streets including large late-medieval timber houses, often subdivided into tenements. The basic street plan is still quite recognisable today, although the centre is now much more densely built up. Notable near the centre of the map are 'Dr Marton's Garden' and the 'Bowling Green'. The former was associated with the Music Room, while the latter belonged to the Sun Inn on Church Street. Both were soon to be built over, in 1785 and 1797 respectively.

Dodshon Foster (1730–93) from a portrait attributed to William Tate and dated *c*.1780. Foster is one of relatively few Lancaster slavers whose portrait has survived. His involvement was fairly brief, between 1752 and 1758, but in this time he transported some 700 slaves to the West Indies.

Lancaster City Museums

London, Liverpool and Bristol, then was finally outlawed. Not, however, before Lancaster men such as Dodshon Foster and Thomas Hinde had made a fortune from slave-trading.

During the course of the eighteenth century a few freed slaves came to Lancaster, mostly travelling as servants to members of ships' crews. Black servants were very fashionable in high society in the early eighteenth century and were often given fancy names, but those who returned to Lancaster seem to have taken their master's name, so apart from these particular church records we cannot identify them from other individuals of local origin. We know of about forty black men and women who appear in the parish registers because they were baptised or buried here. Two are better known than the rest. These are the man known only as 'Sambo', who died in about 1736 and whose grave can be seen on the western shore at Sunderland Point, and John Dixon, a servant at Bare Hall, 'a native Black, from the Island of Grenada', whose tombstone of 1841 stands in Morecambe churchyard. Their lives were very different. The former – so legend tells – died of grief when he thought his master had abandoned him. The latter died aged 75 with over 39 years in honoured domestic service and was commemorated by a tombstone at a time when many servants lay in unmarked graves. Frances Elisabeth Johnson, aged 27 in 1778, who worked for Mr Satterthwaite at 20 Castle Park, is one of the few black women servants to be recorded.[17]

Slavery

Lancaster enjoys the unenviable feature of having briefly in the 1750s been the fourth most important port in England for the slave trade. Slaving voyages at this time were carried out in quite small vessels, some of no more than 50 tons. It was known as 'the Triangular Trade' because ships set off from home ports loaded with manufactured and trade goods – pots and pans, beads, trinkets etc. – for West Africa. Here the were exchanged for slaves brought down from the interior by slave-merchants. The slaves were then transported, often in grossly unhealthy and overcrowded conditions, kept below decks most of the time for fear of riot, and sold in the West Indies and America. The cash received from the sale was then used to purchase a return cargo. Consequently, and contrary to popular imagination, the slaves did not return to Britain. A few former slaves came back with ships' crews, and were regarded as free when they reached this country, especially if they were baptised. Many of the former slaves took names which cannot be distin-guished from the rest of the population, and most must have gradu-ally merged into local society. We only know of those whom the baptism or burial registers identify as 'black'; there may have been many others.

In 1807 the slave trade was abolished in this country, and in the rest of the Empire in 1834. Before the end of the eighteenth century the trade had focused on a few ports such as Liverpool, Bristol and London. Lancaster merchants had either transferred their interests there, or found a new trade. The mid-eighteenth-century prosperity of Lancaster and many of its fine buildings, however, are a direct legacy of the slave trade.

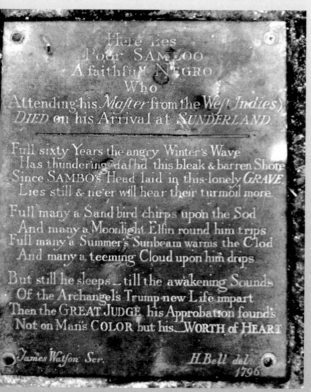

left The brass inscription on Sambo's Grave at Sunderland Point, with verses composed in 1796 by the Master of the Free School, some sixty years after Sambo's death. This is virtually all that is certainly known of him, although folklore supplies a number of the gaps.

below Tombstone of John Dixon in Poulton churchyard, More-cambe. A 'native Black from the Island of Grenada', he died in 1841 after many years of service to the Lodge family of Bare Hall.

CHAPTER FOUR

Visitors

In the Georgian period two factors made travel in Britain more popular than it had been before. The first was improved roads and transport; the second the closing off, through war, of large parts of Europe, forcing those Britons who could afford it to explore their own country instead. From 1750–51 new turn-pike roads were set up which served Lancaster, linking it respectively to Preston and the south and to Kendal and the north (Garstang and Heron Syke Turnpike), and Richmond and the Great North Road (Lancaster and Rich-mond Turnpike). A further road from Carnforth to Ulverston, around the head of Morecambe Bay, followed in 1818–20. Lancaster's position on the main west-coast road to Scotland had long brought traffic through it. Sometimes this was unwelcome traffic, as in 1715 and 1745 when the Jacobite armies passed through.

As the eighteenth century wore on more and faster coaches came through the town, making it a natural place to stay the night and increasing the demand for accommodation. The King's Arms was now the principal inn, the old George having gone into decay, but the Sun Inn on Church Street and the Royal Oak and Commercial Inns in Market Square also did good business with travellers, who left descriptions or comments. Joseph Taylor came here in 1705 on his way to Edinburgh.[18]

> ... about nine we arriv'd at Lancaster, and set up at the Sun, where we lay all night.

Lady Oxford stayed at the same inn in 1745:[19]

> ... thence fourteen miles to Lancaster to the 'Sun', a good Inn.

Her comments are matched by those of John Crofts in 1759:[20]

> The Sun is a very decent inn ...

Mr Monson stayed at the King's Arms in 1816:[21]

> ... The Inn at Lancaster is the King's Arms, very good & civil attendance; they have a curious custom in Lancashire beside the dinner

ordered they load the table with all the productions of the house, cold meat, fowls, tarts &c &c without charge for it cheaper than one dish costs in town.

Benjamin Newton also stayed here in 1818:[22]

... We arrived at the King's Arms, the most magnificent inn in appearance of any we have entered since we left home.

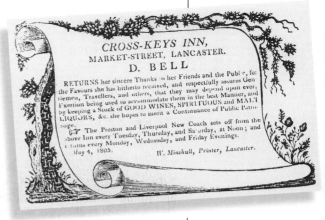

Handbill for D. Bell, innkeeper at the Cross Keys in 1805. The Cross Keys was an early seventeenth-century building at the south west end of Market Street, where British Home Stores now stands. Mrs Bell had probably recently taken over the inn on the death of her husband.

Soulby Collection, Cumbria Record Office, Barrow-in-Furness

In 1814 two coaches left Lancaster each morning for the north and two coaches each afternoon for the south. Cooper's and Dunn's, both coach-builders, were the Lancaster proprietors, handling all the horses. As late as 1846 two long boards showing the times of departure of the coaches were still standing by the side of the Old Sir Simon's Inn in Market Street, which had become the main coaching inn during the last days of the road.[23]

Inns were plentiful. Richard Bond, writing in 1891, was able to list no fewer than 47 in Lancaster which had *closed* in his lifetime, i.e. since c. 1820.[24] Apart from travellers, they catered for people visiting the Assizes and farmers attending the markets and fairs. For these all rooms in the house would be commandeered for dining at a series of 'ordinaries' (set menus at a common table), while stabling would be equally crowded. Many visitors commented on the difficulty of finding accommodation if they arrived at such times. The poet Thomas Gray, visiting in 1769, was one such:[25]

Woe is me! when I got thither, it was the second day of their fair; the inn, in the principal street, was a great old gloomy house, full of people; but I found tolerable quarters, and even slept two nights in peace ...

Surviving records such as probate inventories and the Rule Book of the Borough Court illustrate many examples of Lancaster inns, listing the rooms and their furnishings in some detail. Here is an example from the Rule Book, concerning the White Lion in Penny Street in 1804.

[Borough Rule Book 1784–1822, f.76.]

Samuel Dixon, Samuel Fielding and Joseph Hadwen against Mary Ellershaw, 24th May 1804. It is ordered by this Court that unless the Defendant appear and put in good Bail to this Action within fourteen Days from the date hereof, Sale shall be made of the following Goods and Chattels, to wit, *In the Front Parlour*, one Oak Dining Table, one Deal Dining Table, one Mahogany Stand, one Deal Buffet, three Bowls with one set of Cups and Saucers, three three [sic] Chairs and one

Arm'd one, Dressing Iron, Scales, Smoothing blanket, five Spitting Boxes, two Window Seat Cussions, *In The Kitchen* Dresser, Clock and Case, a Dozen and a half of Plates, ten Dishes, one Sopha, three Chairs, Seven Brass Candlesticks, four Iron ones, Fire Irons and Fender, one Tin Tea Kettle, toasting Iron, one Mahogany Waiter, one Warming Pan,

Dunald Mill Hole at Nether Kellet, a few miles north east of Lancaster, from an engraving by R. Sands after G. Pickering. This romantic limestone cave was very much to the taste of travellers who were directed to it by Christopher Clark in his *Historical & Descriptive Account of the Town of Lancaster* in 1807. The caves and potholes of West Yorkshire were already well known.

Smoothing Irons and Heater, one Oven, *In the Barr* three Plated Pints, one Tankard, Six Ale Glasses, two Pewter Quarts, one Pint, Liquor Measures of all sorts, one Bare Tub, four Waiters, five Case Bottles, one Desk, seven Jugs, one looking Glass, three Punch Ladles, one chest, one Funnel, one Hanging Candlestick, *In Back Kitchen* one Jack, Nine Dishes, twelve Delf Plates, Brown Mugs and Pots, Eight Pickle Pots, Loaf Tin, two Iron Pans, Knife Box, Copper Boiler, Cloaths Wisket, one pair of Bellows, Baking Utensils, Table Cloth, four Chairs, fender and fire Irons, *In the Second Front Parlour* one Dale Table, one Mahogany Card Table, nine Chairs, one Mahogany Dining Table, one Looking Glass, Window Cussions, Fire Irons and Fender, three Pictures, the Bells, and two Window Blinds, of the Goods of the said Defendant.

Many visitors were on their way to see the beauties of the Lake District which was being opened up, by the 1760s and 1770s, as a fashionable tourist destination. Others went to see the picturesque caves and potholes of the Yorkshire Dales. Lancaster was convenient for both, and it was considered by far the best approach to the Lake District to cross the sands of Morecambe Bay from Hest Bank.[26] Lancaster's setting was itself regarded as picturesque, especially the view from Belle Vue on the Greaves with Castle and church silhouetted against the mountains of the Lake District, or the view westwards towards Morecambe Bay from the churchyard. An anonymous visitor in 1764 comments;[27]

> From this [the Castle] you have a most extensive view of the main ocean & river on the left hand with a large tract of corn fields & meadows adorned with gentlemen's seats many miles distance.

Mr Noble recorded in 1774;[28]

> ... towards evening walked to a Hill called Bell View ... where was a fine view of the Sea, the Isle of Man, & several ships at a great distance, the Tide was coming in, upon the Sands which we came over yesterday, which caused a great Addition to the prospect from the said Hill.

There were also many sights in its neighbourhood which appealed to tourists in search of the Picturesque, such as Crook O'Lune near Caton, Dunald Mill Hole near Nether Kellet, or Hornby Castle.[29] With the building of Skerton Bridge in 1788 and the opening of the celebrated canal aqueduct in 1797 new attractions for artists and tourists immediately became popular. The classical style of these bridges and the sylvan landscape of the Lune valley were seen as reminiscent of the Roman countryside which had been popularised by the paintings of Claude Lorraine, Salvator Rosa and Nicholas Poussin, all tremendously influential figures in the creation of the 'ideal' Romantic land-scape. Mr Monson wrote in 1816:[30]

> After Dinner walked to Mr Grays famous view of the Vale of Lonsdale the road runs under the Lancaster Canal I think in seeing this view, beautiful as it is, there is one defect – the station is not sufficiently elevated we might perhaps not have found the right place, for the gate mentioned by West no longer exists. Ingleborough is a most noble back ground to the scene – in returning Lancaster Castle &c breaks upon you finely in turning the hill through the archway over which the canal runs. We got duck'd in our return by two or three showers but the Evening while we were at the view was very prosperous.
>
> ... Walk'd up again to Lancaster Hill, the scenery towards inland with the noble view of the Aqueduct over the Lune put me in mind of some of Claude's Italian Landscapes. The tide was up, which shewed the river to advantage ...

A number of important artists from Farington to Turner made use of these viewpoints for their paintings.

Public Life

There were very few paid offices at a local level in the Georgian period. Men who had reached a point in their working lives where they had a little more time, such as those who had reliable apprentices to run their businesses, would often undertake some unpaid office. Typical of this would be service on the Corporation or on the parish church vestry (which undertook a huge range of duties now performed by local government or the state). Quakers and other nonconformists, as well as Catholics, might take on duties within their own church, finding a use for energy and talents that the state thought it could manage without. Women of ability also found themselves in this position. They might also find a natural place organising charities, such as those for lying-in (childbirth) or relief of prisoners.

right The Town Hall and Market Square engraved by Rawle after Westall, 1829. A market of sorts is in progress and the iron gates enclosing the corn market can be seen on the ground floor of the building. On the right is the Commercial Inn, built in 1799 and one of the principal coaching inns of the town.

Lancaster City Museums

TO all and singular Justices and Keepers of the Peace, Sheriffs, Mayors, Aldermen Bailiffs, Constables, and other Officers, Ministers, and faithful Liege Subjects of our Lord the King, to whom these Presents shall come *I James Hinde* Esq; Mayor of the Borough or Town of *Lancaster*, in the County of *Lancaster*, Greeting, in our Lord God everlasting. Know ye, that the said Borough of *Lancaster* is an ancient Borough, and that all the Burgesses thereof have and enjoy, and for time immemorial have and enjoyed the Liberties, Privileges, and Immunities to be exonerated and acquitted of all Toll, Passage-Toll, Bridge-Toll, Stallage, Poundage. Tonage, Lastage, and also of all other Exactions and Demands whatsoever, for all their Wares and Merchandizes bought or sold throughout the whole Kingdom of *England*, as also through every Sea-port and Islands, Cities, Ports, and Towns of *Ireland, Wales*, or *Man*; and which our Lord *James* the First, late King of *England, Scotland, France*, and *Ireland*, by his Letters Patent under the great Seal of *England*, granted and confirmed to his Burgesses of his Borough aforesaid, and their Successors for ever, the Liberties, Privileges, and Immunities aforesaid, according to the Tenor of divers Charters of the Ancestors and Predecessors of our said Lord the King, to the same Burgesses and their Successors, granted from the time of the Reign of the late King *John*, and by our Lord *Charles* the Second, late King of *England, Scotland, France* and *Ireland*, to the same Burgesses by his Letters Patent, and Charters lately confirmed as by the said Letters Patents, Charters and Powers remaining with the said Burgesses, will more fully and at large appear. Which said Premises I not only testify to you by the Tenor of these Presents, but also that *George Harrison of Appleby in the County of Westmorland Gentleman* is a Burgess admitted and Sworn to the Liberties of the same Borough or Vill of *Lancaster* aforesaid. Wherefore I the aforesaid Mayor, specially require whenever the said *George Harrison* or his Servants shall come to the Cities, Ports, Towns, or other Places within the Kingdom of *England*, or to the Ports and Islands of *Ireland, Wales* or *Man*, with his Goods, Wares or Merchandizes that he and they shall be freed and acquitted of all Passage-Toll, Bridge-Toll, Stallage, Poundage, Tonage, Lastage, and all other Exactions according to the Grants aforesaid. In witness whereof to these Presents, I the aforesaid Mayor have put the Seal of my Office, this *Fourth* Day of *August* in the *Twenty third* Year of the Reign of our Most Gracious Sovereign Lord *George* the Third by the Grace of God, of *Great Britain, France*, and *Ireland*, King, Defender of the Faith and so forth, and in the Year of our Lord one Thousand Seven Hundred and *Eighty three (1783)*

left Letters patent, dated 1783 and signed by the Mayor, James Hinde, declaring the privileges of a Freeman of Lancaster awarded to George Harrison of Appleby, Gentleman. Although the ability to trade in one's home town after a seven years' apprenticeship was important, by the end of the eighteenth century many merchants were finding the reciprocal freedom from toll in certain other cities equally valuable, and many outsiders bought their freedom because of its advantages, including a vote in parliamentary elections.

Lancaster City Museums

The Corporation, until it was reformed in 1835, was a small and self-perpetuating elite of the local merchants and tradesmen who were Freemen of the borough by apprenticeship or by purchase. Women were not represented on it at all. Unlike modern local government, it did not regard itself as having any duty towards the local community, with services paid for from rates. It really represented only the interests of the Freemen, who increasingly during the eighteenth century ceased to have any real relevance to the wider town and its needs. With the growth of commerce the medieval concept of a closed town, controlling its own trades and having little contact with anywhere else, was breaking down. Increasingly merchants had interests in several towns and cities, as well as abroad. The prosperity also attracted non-residents, who were not interested in the long-term position of freeman.

At the head of the Corporation were the Mayor – elected annually in October – seven aldermen and twenty-four members of the common council. After 1819 the latter were divided into 'capital burgesses' and 'common councilmen', twelve of each. Two Bailiffs, elected from the Corporation, oversaw all income and expenditure, which roughly balanced, and averaged about £800 each year for much of the eighteenth century. The Corporation records reveal how little business was done in average years. Elections and junkets, an occasional loyal address, a lawsuit or two in protection of the

Allowed the said Bailiffs.

	L.	s	d
Allowed the said Bailiffs by them paid the Fee Farm Rent of the Town to Mr Ashurst	13	6	8
Allowed them paid the said Mr Ashurst the Fee Farm Rent of the Copyholds	2	10	—
Allowed them paid for Fees and Wages, to wit, To Mr Mayor 42. To the Bailiffs 2:0:0. To the Clerk 1:5:0. To the Serjeant at Mace 6:8. To the Bellman 2:0. To the Macebearer 1:6:8	47	—	4
Allowed them paid Mr Recorder's Salary	2	2	
Allowed them paid for Liveries	33	5	5½
Allowed them paid as appears by the Libol	60	10	11½
Allowed them paid for Sealing Measures		13	4
Allowed them paid for Collecting Rents and Acquittances as usual		4	—
Allowed them paid the Almsmen	2	4	—
Allowed them paid the Beadle for Ringing the Fish Market Bell &c		17	7
Allowed them paid the Swineherd			
Allowed them paid Assessments upon the Town and for Tolls and Toll Houses	25	3	9
Allowed them paid Expences above the Libel	3	10	—
Allowed them paid the Overseers of the Poor the Interest of Sir John Harrison's Legacy	5	—	—
Allowed them paid the Head School Master's Salary	30	—	
Allowed them paid the Augmentation of his Salary	4	10	—
Allowed them paid him the Interest of Mr Procter's Legacy		10	—
Allowed them paid the Carter of Kent Sands		2	6
Allowed them paid the Serjeants and Bellman in Lieu of their Nights	6	—	—
Allowed them paid for Repairs and Paving	199	10	4½
Allowed them paid Expences on the Auditors		8	—
Allowed them paid Expences on Driving the Moor	2	4	10
Allowed them paid for Oil, Candles and for Lighting and Repairing the Lamps	93	8	9½
Carried over	519	12	

A typical page of the Bailiffs' Accounts, rendered at the end of their year of office, this one dating from the 1770s. The details would have been kept in rough books, a neater version supplied for auditing, and then a summary written up in the borough minutes. The last of these is usually the only surviving version. The 'Libel' referred to has nothing to do with defamation, but is 'libellum', Latin for a little book, meaning essentially petty cash. Much of the expenditure went on from year to year unchanged and was kept at a minimal level. Noteworthy is the payment to the Carter of Kent Sands, the guide to the sands of Morecambe Bay.

Lancaster Borough Records

Borough of *Lancaster* 25th. of November 1767.

THE Days appointed for the admiſſion of Freemens Sons and Apprentices who have ſerved a ſeven Years Apprenticeſhip to Freemen, within the Town of LANCASTER, are the 14th. and 21ſt. Days of January next, at nine o'Clock in the Forenoon of each Day, when each Freeman's Son intending to take up his Freedom, is to bring his Father, or ſome other Perſon along with him, to prove that he is duly qualified to take up his Freedom. And each Freeman's Apprentice is to produce his Indenture, and bring his Maſter (if living) or if Dead, ſome other credible Perſon along with him into Court, to certify that he has faithfully ſerved his Apprenticeſhip of ſeven Years.

above Notice of the annual Freemen's Court to be held by the borough in January 1768. Admission to the ranks of 'Freeman' was open to sons of Freemen, those who had undertaken an apprenticeship to a Freeman, those who would pay a 'fine' for the privilege, as well as those few whom the borough wished to honour by the gift of Freedom of the city. Apart from the benefits of being able to trade in Lancaster, Freemen had the right to vote in parliamentary elections.
Lancaster Central Library

body's interests, and that was all. Income came mainly from tolls and from leasing out of land in the Corporation's ownership. This became more important as the town grew on to what had been waste land, over which the Corporation exercised a proprietary interest. Expenditure was very limited, because there were no regular rates to support its work, but often included legal bills for defending the Corporation's rights.

Freemen had certain benefits. They could gain freedom from toll in many other mercantile towns and cities, a valuable right for merchants which was enshrined in a small piece of parchment signed by the Mayor. Only they and property owners could vote in national elections for the town's MPs. Eighteenth-century elections were usually squalid and violent affairs, with wholesale bribery, while mobs, drunk on free alcohol, terrorised ordinary citizens. Local aristocratic landowners usually effectively controlled the parliamentary seats and in Lancaster would pay for their servants or tenants to become Freemen in order to acquire sufficient votes for their chosen candidates. Thus in election years the number of men buying their Freedom – non-resident Freemen – rose very steeply. This had very little to do with the resident exercise of the Freedom enjoyed principally by those who had undergone an apprenticeship, a medieval tradition which was being eroded from all sides by the late eighteenth century as horizons widened and people became more mobile.

There were a few large items of expenditure in the later eighteenth century. The New Shambles was built for the town's butchers in the 1770s (it has disappeared without trace, but can be seen on Mackreth's map on page 20) and from 1781–83 the building of the new Town Hall (now the City Museum) cost a little over £2,000. The Bailiffs presented their accounts at the end of each year and the list is extremely repetitive. Ancient tolls, fines from new Burgesses and the Stallenge, periodic rentals of the wastes or the Shambles (the latter bringing in about £200) and that was about it. Most accounts run to a couple of pages. Expenditure was correspondingly confined and repetitive, with wages for a handful of public servants, and included costs attributed to the Free School, such as the salaries of the master and the cost of books. The Borough Court, held every Thursday, dealt with most of the minor disputes between freemen. Its records are now an extremely useful source for social history.

Lancaster Corporation was not as corrupt or self-indulgent as many. Bristol, for instance, was a byeword for junketing and disregard of other interests,[31] but a frustration began to build up with the sort of dead hand which lay upon the administration even of Lancaster. Much local energy was diverted into the Port Commission, formed in 1749 with a membership of shipowners, which ran the port and the navigation of the Lune. It built St George's Quay in 1750

Built in 1781–83 the Old Town Hall was a rather late response by the Corporation to the increasing prosperity of the town. Up to that date they had been content with a ramshackle building of the 1670s which lacked facilities for the most basic services, which meant that most Corporation business other than formal meetings was carried out in inns. Even as rebuilt the new structure contained a corn market on its ground floor and its cellars were let out as shops.

and New Quay, further downriver, in 1767. It was also responsible for the creation of Glasson Dock at the mouth of the river in the 1780s and building and maintaining the lighthouse at the south end of Walney Island, which guarded the entrance into Morecambe Bay, in 1790 and thereafter. This was typical of the way in which corporations became moribund while functions of public interest were taken over by others. In the same way the Police Commissioners of 1824 – the title is a little misleading, since policing was only part of their work – took on many tasks which we would now consider the duty of a local authority, such as paving and lighting the streets. Their actions were in many ways a sign of public exasperation at the irrelevance of the Corporation, and membership included many of those who were excluded from that body.

Lancaster Corporation

We tend to look upon borough corporations as having some democratic role in running local affairs, but this was not true in the Georgian period. Corporations such as that of Lancaster were made up of Freemen, either by apprenticeship or by gift or purchase, and were dedicated, if that is the right word, to upholding their own benefits and privileges. Any thought of service to the wider community was of secondary importance. The Corporation owned certain property and had the right to extract tolls on goods passing through and upon certain other things. Its income was modest, and so was its expenditure. It did not look for new activities or responsibilities. Most of its work was carried out by a small group of office-holders, led by the Mayor and two Bailiffs, elected each year in October. The Town Clerk was one of the few paid officers, along with the Master of the Free School, for which the Corporation was responsible.

Even the reforms of 1835 had little effect on the democratic or service elements. Great frustration developed over the 'dead hand' of the Corporation, which would not undertake new things in a changing world, but resisted anyone else doing them. In 1749 the Lancaster Port Commission was created by Act of Parliament allowing a group of merchants to create the conditions for an effective port, while in 1824 the Police Act allowed a new group of commissioners to carry out functions of law and order as well as lighting, paving etc. The shortcomings of the Corporation, which had not been of great significance in the seventeenth century, became an increasingly serious issue in the eighteenth century, at a time when fundamental changes were affecting most towns and trades.

Low Life

Georgian England suffered a relatively low level of crime by modern standards, apart from certain times of famine when some poor people turned to theft or poaching to feed their families. London was recognised as having by far the biggest crime problem, with a criminal underworld, but a country town such as Lancaster survived until 1824 without any regular means of law enforcement, other than the Town Sergeant. His powers were limited and usually involved locking suspects away in the so-called 'Black Hole' under the main stairs of the Town Hall, pending a hearing at the borough court which was held weekly on a Thursday. A portrait[32] of one Georgian Town Sergeant, Robert Harrison, who died aged 79 in 1851, has come down to us. He is also immortalised by the local poet William Sanderson,[33] who wrote;

> *Robert Harrison, so round and fat,*
> *In all the pride of his gold-trimmed laced*
>   *cocked hat.*

The fact that most people in the town knew each other's business meant that it was quite hard to get away with felony, while mobility had not yet increased to the point where much of a threat was represented by professional criminals. Drunkenness and petty theft were the commonest crimes, and cases of the latter stood a good chance of being solved, except in the turmoil of race meetings, where strangers were commonplace and where cash and watches regularly disappeared.

This is not to say that there was not a huge amount of litigation in the borough courts. Going to law seems to have been a very popular practice in Georgian Lancaster, but we should remember that there was much less government regulation then than now and often the only remedy for petty

Broadsheet listing sentences of Crown prisoners, dated 1823. When the Assizes were ended these lists would be rushed out by the printers, who had a ready trade among local people. Before leaving Lancaster, however, it was quite common for judges to remit sentences of death or reduce them to transportation or imprisonment, so the printed lists cannot always be trusted. This list already has some late reprieves marked but in fact 1823 was unusual in having no executions at all, so William Hopkinson snr was also subsequently reprieved.

Lancaster City Museums

left Portrait of Robert Harrison, Town's Sergeant and for all practical purposes the representative of law in Lancaster from the late eighteenth century until the 'Watch' and later the borough police were created. Increased mobility and better transport made the old ways increasingly untenable. The sort of policing which Harrison could do was robust and physical, though probably requiring few detective skills.

Lancaster City Museums

FULL

Sentences,

OF ALL THE

Crown Prisoners,

Confined in His Majesty's Gaol, at Lancaster,
**Who have taken their Trials at the August
Assizes, commencing on the 13th, 1823.**

Thomas Green, Esq., Sheriff.

Salford Hundred.

Jeremia Higginbottom, 76, charged with killing and slaying James Walters, at Manchester—14 Days Imprisonment.

Thomas Griffiths, 23, and Thomas Lea, 19, charged with robbing John Brittain at Salford.—*Death. reprieved.*

John Rothwell, 22, and Edmund Taylor, 20, charged with killing Samuel Yate, at Bury.—2 Years Imprisonment.

David Charlesworth, 18, and John Walker, 26, charged with robbing John Rothwell, at Rochdale, *Acquitted*

James Ingham, 18, and James Whitworth, 21, charged with robbing John Fernaley, at Hyde, *Death reprieved.*

Johnathan Crowder, 25, and William Jackson 20, charged with stealing a gelding, at Manchester, *Death reprieved.*

John Holden, 17, charged with killing Hugh Chesworth, at Manchester.—*Acquitted.*

Charlotte Redfey alias Saumarez, 28, charged with bigamy.—*Acquitted.*

West Derby and Leyland Hundreds.

John Lyon, 25, charged with stealing a gelding, at Liverpool.—*Death reprieved.*

John Rothwell, 37, charged with having unnatural dealings with a mare, at Liverpool.—*Acquitted.*

James Hinton, 30, charged with cutting and maiming John Swift, at West Derby, with intent to do him some grievous bodily harm.—*Acquitted.*

Richard Robinson, 24, charged with having broken into the dwelling house of William Greaves, at Liverpool, and stealing money and other articles.—*Death reprieved.*

Robert Woolfall, 27, charged with receiving money knowing the same to be stolen, the property of William C ares.—*No Prosecution.*

Thomas Ashton, 15, charged with having broken into the dwelling house of John Callwood, at Liverpool, and stealing several articles.—*Death reprieved.*

John Jolly, 34, charged with uttering a counterfeit bill of exchange, at Chorley.—*Acquitted.*

William Rosbottom, 42, charged with having uttered several forged warrants, for the delivery of goods, with an intent to defraud Randolp Perswick and William Bone, of Ashton.—1 Year Imp.

Samuel Prescot, 48, charged with having ravished and carnally known Margaret Chadwick, at Westleigh.—*No Bill.*

William Lathom, 35, charged with killing Edmund Gaskell, at Upholland.—3 Years Imprisonment.

Joao Roisno Da Silva, 39, charged with uttering a forged bill of Exchange. at Liverpool.—*No bill.*

Lonsdale, Amounderness, and Blackburn. Hundreds.

William Hopkinson, the elder, 63, and William Hopkinson, the younger, 27, charged with having uttered several counterfeit notes, with intent to defraud various persons.—*Sen. Death, Jun. Acquit.*

John Shuttleworth, 22, charged with stealing at Colne, a quantity of cloth, &c.—2 Years Imp.

William Greenwood, 27, charged with selling a quantity of woollen cord, knowing the same to be stolen. at Colne.—*Admitted Evidence.*

Henry Cansfield, 48, Charged with having broken into the dwelling house of John Western, at Yealand Redmayne, and stealing various articles.—*Acquitted.*

Andrew Ryding, charged with having at Preston, wilfully and maliciously cut, with a cleaver, Samuel Horrocks, Esqr. with intent to murder him.—*Not Guilty. on account of insanity, but to remain in custody till his Majesty's pleasure.*

Edward Sumner, for Manslaughter, at Liverpool.—3 Months Imp

Peter Bretherton, for Manslaughter.—*Acquitted.*

Thomas Wardle, 40, charged with killing John Booth, at Hutton.—*Acquitted.*

Thomas Hall, charged with the wilful murder of Thomas Cowan, at Rochdale.—*Acquitted.*

J. M'CORNACK, PRINTER, 179, FRIARGATE, PRESTON.

infringements and annoyances was recourse to the courts. Besides, the courts were also seen as a means of getting matters into the official record, and might be used for all sorts of purposes other than what appeared on the surface to be the case. What show up as fines should often be seen in the light of licences, with no stigma attached.

However, Lancaster was the county town, and Lancashire in Georgian times – a primary area for the birth of the Industrial Revolution – was rapidly becoming one of the most densely populated and lawless areas in Europe. One reason was that it rapidly outgrew the ancient means of preserving the peace and nothing adequate was put in its place until the mid-nineteenth century. This meant that criminal cases from all over Lancashire were tried here in Lancaster. The Assizes were held twice each year and suspected criminals were held in the Castle pending trial. Prison was not on the whole used as a punishment in itself. It was mainly used as a place to hold suspects pending trial. Convicted criminals could be flogged, branded in the hand, transported or hanged. Minor offences might lead to a period of custody in the House of Correction. Hanging could be inflicted for what we would see as petty crimes, such as passing fake banknotes or the theft of clothes. There were in consequence nearly two hundred capital offences on the statute book, although in practice leniency often prevailed. Many criminals sentenced to death at the Assizes had their sentences commuted before the justices left town, while it seems that the courts often leaned over backwards to avoid convicting on the less obviously serious of the capital offences on the statute book. A case in point is that of Thomas Robinson, convicted of Highway Robbery at the Lancaster Assizes of 1803, who received sentence of death. This was commuted to transportation for life to the eastern coast of New South Wales shortly afterwards but within a couple of months the sentence was once again reduced to imprisonment for one year! He was a lucky man, although his case is probably not all that unusual.[34]

Louis Simond, a French-American visitor in 1810, had this to say:[35]

... The old castle has been turned into a prison and court-house, the arrangement nearly on the plan of Chester, and owing likewise to the active humanity of Howard; it is even better than the one at Chester, as there is more room. The number of prisoners, however, we were sorry to see much greater, criminals as well as debtors. The jailor said he had under his lock and key debtors from £45,000 (a delinquent, collector of the customs) to seven shillings. Debtors for less than £10, we were told, are let out without cost, after as many days detention as there are shillings in the sum they owe; the creditor is obliged to pay for their maintenance. There are ten or twelve criminals executed every year,

Lancaster Castle, Court House, and Church, 1833, engraved by T. Higham after T. Allom. It shows the arrival of the High Sheriff, with his escort of javelin-men, perhaps for the ceremony of Shield-Hanging. Each year the new High Sheriff hung a small version of his shield of arms on the inner wall of the Shire Hall. Another duty was to meet and escort the Circuit Judges to the Assizes.

and a greater number transported to Botany Bay, who do not consider it as any punishment at all. Some are kept here at hard labour, something on the plan of our penitentiary prisons in America …

A German visitor, Dr S. H. Spiker, made these observations in 1816:[36]

… Among the objects worth seeing here, the castle claims the first place … From the thronged state of the prison, instead of only sixteen or seventeen persons, which these rooms were originally intended to contain, twenty-six persons now slept in them, which is calculated to render the atmosphere of the rooms very unwholesome. From the top of the tower we looked down into the court of the prison, and were enabled to form a distinct idea of its internal arrangement. Each tower has its own peculiar division of the court in front of it, enclosed by a wall, in which the prisoners may walk at stated times, without having any communication with the prisoner of the other towers. The ground in these divisions is flagged, that it may always be kept clean, and a well supplies the prisoners with water during their walk. The two towers next to Adrian's tower, contain forty cells each; and a new one, which will contain room for 120 women, was building, for the which, alas, the beautiful Gothic tower beside it was to be demolished! The number of persons confined in the different receptacles was considerable, even for a county of the extent of Lancaster; there at this time 197 male and 53 female criminals, and 150 debtors, amounting in all to 400 persons. Of the former, 34 men and 11 women were sentenced to transportation, and on 17 no sentence had yet been passed ...

Until 1800 hangings took place on a temporary gallows set up on Lancaster Moor. From that date they were transferred to a new site behind the Castle, at a place which became known as 'Hanging Corner'. Executions usually took place within a few days of sentence and often a number of criminals would be hanged at once. This was considered a public spectacle and spectators would travel in large numbers from south or east Lancashire to witness the event, if the hangings represented crimes from those areas. The Master of the nearby Free Grammar School in the churchyard, Rev. Joseph Rowley (Usher 1794–1802, Master 1802–12), would often give the boys the day off to watch executions, on the principle that they would learn the ways of righteousness. Unfortunately, there is no evidence to suggest that watching public executions had the slightest effect on crime. If anything those executed often seem to have gained a spurious glamour from their brief moment of fame, and meanwhile pickpockets worked the watching crowds.

The Quakers' Room, the best of the many debtors' rooms in the Castle, engraved by Edward Slack in 1836. Debtors could be held here for years. Boredom was the main enemy. Some of the debtors could live quite well, provided they had friends or family on the outside who took care of them.

AN

A C T

FOR

Lighting, watching, paving, cleansing, and improving the Streets, Highways, and Places within the Borough and Town of *Lancaster,* in the County Palatine of *Lancaster.*

[ROYAL ASSENT, 28th May, 1824.]

WHEREAS the Borough and Town of Lancaster, in the Preamble. County Palatine of Lancaster, is populous, and a Place of Trade, and is also a great Thoroughfare for Travellers, and several of the Highways, Markets, Streets, Lanes, Ways, public Passages and Places within the said Borough and Town, are not properly paved, repaired, cleansed, lighted and watched, and are subject to various Nuisances, Annoyances, Encroachments, and Obstructions, and it would tend to the Protection and Preservation of the Lives and Property of the Inhabitants of the said Borough and Town, and to all Persons resorting to and travelling through the same if the said Highways, Markets, Streets, Lanes, Ways, Passages, and Places were properly paved, repaired, cleansed, lighted, and watched, and the Nuisances and Annoyances, Obstructions and Encroachments therein were removed and prevented, and proper Fire Engines and Firemen provided therein for the future ; but as the several Purposes aforesaid cannot be effected without the Aid and Authority of Parliament ;

May it therefore please your MAJESTY,

That it may be enacted, and BE IT ENACTED by the KING's Most Excellent MAJESTY, by and with the Advice and Consent
A   of

A local Act of Parliament for lighting, paving and watching the streets, dated 1824. This was the first step towards modern public services paid for from the rates. These services had been available before, but paid for privately and not for the benefit of all. The Corporation at this period was more or less moribund and did not see itself as having any duty to anyone except Freemen. The most important outcome was the creation of so-called 'Police' Commissioners with wide duties. The Watch, while laughably inefficient, made way for the borough's own police force after the 1835 reforms of local government.

Most of the prisoners in the Castle were debtors, who could be held indefinitely for a debt of as little as £2. They were held until they could pay their debts, which might mean for life. Late in the eighteenth century a law was passed allowing small debtors without any other crime to their name to go free, but up to 500–600 debtors lived in the Castle at any one time, as well as both male and female felons. Consequently it was extremely crowded. Debtors were accommodated in the Lungess Tower, the Gatehouse, and in numerous other places, all with distinctive names. Where you lodged, and how well, depended on how much you paid the gaoler (a fee, known as 'entrance money' was paid on arrival). Many poor debtors practised a trade while confined, such as tailoring or bootmaking, serving other prisoners and an outside market. Painting and sketching were popular pastimes, and some debtors may have emerged from their ordeal as accomplished artists. Among these was Gideon Yates, who entered debtors' prison as a failed marine insurance broker in 1804 and emerged as a professional artist in 1805. Many of his watercolours can be seen in the City Museum.

After the Napoleonic Wars, which ended with Waterloo in 1815, there was widespread suffering when many thousands of soldiers and sailors were discharged and thrown onto the streets. This was accompanied by worries that new machinery was taking away traditional jobs in spinning and weaving. Radical groups sprang up and the authorities crushed riots and demonstrations alike with great savagery, using the army and yeomanry. After the Peterloo Massacre of 1819 some of the principal radicals, such as 'Orator' Hunt and Samuel Bamford, were brought to Lancaster Castle for holding, presumably as far from radical Manchester as possible.[37]

Many towns found crime and violence increasing and Lancaster was one which applied for a 'Police' Act, in 1824. This was not just about policing as we understand it but also covered paving and lighting of the streets. One effect, though, was the setting up of a Watch with constables who patrolled the streets especially during winter nights. They were popularly known as 'Charleys' and though not very effective they were the first organised law and order in the town. The first superintendent of the Watch was Richard Hogarth, whose successor survived the reform of local government in 1835 to become the first superintendent of the Borough Police. The Watch had boxes

in Dalton Square and at Queen Square to which they retired between patrols. Richard Bond, writing in 1891 of his childhood, remembers the Watch calling out 'past ten o'clock, a fine moonlight night', as they patrolled the streets. He also recalls them being plagued by 'young bloods', who would sing 'Tom and Jerry, Tom and Jerry, we're the lads for kicking up a row', as they returned home drunk. Some things don't change all that much![38]

On the various landed estates outside the town poaching became a significant problem, especially after Waterloo. In years of bad harvest or extreme weather many poor people were driven by hunger to risk the danger of gamekeepers, traps and spring-guns to feed their families this way. On Kirkland Hall estates near Garstang a series of great steel man-traps was set in the 1820s to deter or catch poachers.[39] One of these survives in Lancaster City Museums. Its jaws could shatter a man's leg or cause him to bleed to death. Occasionally pitched battles took place between groups of desperate men and gamekeepers, such as the one at Claughton-on-Brock, the estate of the Fitzherbert Brockholes family. Early in 1827 a group of six poachers were involved in an affray in which the gamekeeper, Francis Whitehead, received gunshot wounds from which he later died. The six, Thomas Varley, James Bleazard, William Marley, Peter Spencer, John Barlow and John Maudsley, were committed to Lancaster Castle. Subsequently Varley and Spencer were transported for seven years; the rest received a sentence of two years'

Man-trap from Kirkland Hall, near Garstang, dating from the most savage implementation of the game laws in the 1820s. It was a period of hunger and want, when gangs of armed poachers openly clashed with gamekeepers and when spring-guns and man-traps such as this, capable of smashing a man's leg or causing him to bleed to death, were laid across known paths on private estates.

Lancaster City Museums

imprisonment.[40] A painting of 'Lancaster Castle with the Arrival of Prisoners', now in Lancaster City Museum, seems to show the Claughton gang being marched into the Castle in manacles, watched by a boisterous crowd. Judging by their clothes and missing limbs several of the gang were ex-soldiers or sailors. The war over game was not a one-way process. A case tried at the same Assizes involved two gamekeepers at Halton who had maliciously shot a man, William Caton, while he was out poaching there. Their death sentence was afterwards commuted to three years' imprisonment.[41]

Crime & Punishment

The Georgian period saw great changes in the pattern of crime in Lancaster. In the early eighteenth century it was mostly petty and local in character, fairly easily managed by the Town Sergeant as constable. By the 1820s easier travel and greater mobility, as well as political unease and unemployment after the Napoleonic Wars meant new systems were required. A Police Act of 1824 established a Watch made up of a handful of constables, which became the basis of the Borough Police Force in 1835.

But most of the criminals tried at Lancaster Castle were from elsewhere in the county, especially from the rapidly developing south and east Lancashire including the recently urbanised Liverpool and Manchester. The policing and

right Irons used for the restraint of prisoners in the Castle and now displayed in Adrian's Tower. Imprisonment was not much used in Georgian times as a punishment. Most prisoners were held only pending trial. The use of irons for condemned or potentially dangerous prisoners was more to do with the lack of gaolers to supervise them.

left One of the cells in the basement of the medieval hall, next to Adrian's Tower in the Castle. Rediscovered and remodelled in the eighteenth century, it gives an unpleasant taste of incarceration to visitors, who are shut in it. The small window over the door is the only source of light and ventilation.

legal systems simply did not keep pace with the growth and lawlessness of these areas. At the twice-yearly Assizes a long list of cases were tried, often leading to executions within the following days. Originally hangings had taken place at 'Tiburn' on Lancaster Moor, but from 1801 they were moved to 'Hanging Corner' at the rear of the Castle. Vast crowds turned out to see them. They varied vastly in numbers, from 11 in 1806, to 13 in 1812 and no fewer than 20 in 1817, while 1823 and 1825 saw no executions at all. In the 1780s an alternative to execution arrived in the form of transportation to Australia. Gradually fewer crimes were seen to merit the death penalty.

Minor offences such as drunkenness could lead to summary imprisonment in the town gaol, in the Town Hall, or to the stocks or pillory in Market Square.

left The chair on wheels made for Jane Scott, who was hanged for the murder of her mother in Preston on 22 March 1828. She was what we would now describe as anorexic, and too weak to walk.

right The so-called 'Hanging Corner' at the rear of the Castle. Originally hangings took place on Lancaster Moor, but from 1801 onwards executions took place here until public hangings ceased.
After each Assize a scaffolding would be constructed outside the round tower and the condemned prisoners would be led through the Grand Jury Room to a specially contrived door in the wall which opened onto the scaffold. Crowds of spectators, including grammar school boys, would gather in the churchyard opposite.

Children's Life

There is good reason to describe the concept of 'childhood' as a Victorian invention. In the Georgian period there was little cult of the child; children were just junior adults. Child mortality was high and families were generally large enough to accommodate the loss of several children before they reached adulthood. In poor families children were a burden until they could make themselves useful by going out to work or running errands – there was no legal minimum age for working until much later. In better-off families child-hood extended from birth to the age of about six or seven, during which time children of both sexes were dressed the same. Boys were 'breeched' (put into breeches) at about six, and thereafter both sexes were treated as miniature adults, wearing smaller versions of adult clothes, although boys and girls thenceforth had very different expectations and upbringing.

For the poor there was all sorts of child labour – assisting in the home, fetching and carrying, looking after livestock (even in the town, since the common fields lay close by), working in the sailcloth or cotton mills, or as domestic servants. Boys might be put out as apprentices from the age of thirteen, and their keep became their master's responsibility. At all events there was no clearly defined period of childhood without responsibility, followed by a different adult world.

For the better-off there was a prospect of schooling, although this was not compulsory and could take many forms. Girls' schooling was directed either at practical domestic training such as sewing, fitting them for domestic service, especially at the Charity School on Fenton Street (opened in 1820), or at producing fashionable and composed young ladies, adept at music, art and polite conversation. Boarding schools of the latter type were also tacitly designed for keeping girls occupied and out of trouble. Boys could gain a classical education – increasingly irrelevant as the century wore on – at the Free School, which stood in the churchyard, or a more commercially directed education involving mathematics and book-keeping at one of the many private academies.

Seven Headmasters of the Free School spanned the Georgian period, which was not exactly the zenith of its reputation. Most of them were in holy orders

Detail from a lithograph by Bedford after Fielding showing the Free School of 1682 which stood on the edge of the churchyard and remained in use throughout the Georgian period, only being replaced by new Grammar School buildings in East Road in 1851.

Lancaster City Museums

and combined the post with that of Chaplain of the Castle or with other livings. They were supported by an usher and later by a writing master. Some of these individuals were men of real talent and lowly origin, such as Rev. James Watson (Master 1765–94) or William Cockin (Writing master 1764–84).[42] By 1818 the Free School had redirected its syllabus to a more modern model. School teaching was one of the few practical jobs for intelligent people of humble origin and was often combined with holy orders or land-surveying. The Rev. William Lamport taught in St Nicholas Street while Edward Howard kept a Mathematical and Philosophical Academy in Pitt Street in the early nineteenth century. Schools for girls were often residential and enabled spinsters or widows to find a viable economic use for a large house. In 1825 Barbara and Mary Shaw had a ladies' boarding school on Castle Hill and a near neighbour, Mrs Catharine Owen (mother of the famous Richard Owen, inventor of

GRAMMAR SCHOOL. LANCASTER.

the concept of 'dinosaur') kept another.[43] Georgina Trusler's school has the distinction of being listed in great detail in the Borough Rule Book[44] as she seems to have got into financial difficulties in 1795. The contents of eleven rooms are listed, including the School Room. The inventory of goods shows 18 delft plates, four bells with pulleys, a quantity of black lead pencils, one hand bell, the contents of school room, three school forms (in the garretts) and personal possessions. From other sources we know that she lived in Back Lane (King St).[45]

There were also several denominational schools, such as the Catholic Charity School next to the Dalton Square chapel, while a Lancasterian School, established in Moor Lane in 1813 and later moved to Aldcliffe Lane, offered a non-denominational education using pupil-teachers. (The system has nothing to do with Lancaster itself but was named after its founder, Joseph Lancaster.) An interesting description of life at the Free School in the 1770s appears in evidence taken from several old scholars such as Thomas Casson, William Wakefield and Joseph Bell, contemporaries of John Marsden, the later owner of Hornby Castle, at the Tatham *vs* Wright Will Cause. It is worth reading the original, because the answers are quite lengthy. Here is one, Joseph Bell, under examination:[46]

Did you go to school at the Free-School? – *Yes.*

Was Mr. Cockin the writing-master? – *Yes, he was.*

Did he teach writing and arithmetic? – *Yes.*

Was the writing-room below? – *No, over the grammar school.*

When did you go to Mr. Cockin's? – *I was there in 1772 and 1773.*

In one of those years when you were there, did John Marsden come to Mr. Cockin as a scholar? – *He did.*

Are you able to say whether Mr. Cockin took pains with him? – *He used to take a great deal of pains with him; he had him opposite to him at his own desk …*

EDUCATION.

EDWARD ADLINGTON,
(Immediately from the Free-Grammar-School of Lancaster, where he has been regularly educated)
ENCOURAGED BY THE APPLICATIONS OF HIS FRIENDS,
Propoſes opening a SCHOOL *for teaching*
Engliſh, Latin, Writing, Arithmetic, Book-keeping, &c.
On MONDAY *the 27th of May next,*
In the old Concert Room behind the Horſe and Farrier, Church-Street; and hopes by his Ability, Care & Diligence to merit the Patronage of the Public.

TERMS.

Engliſh & Latin - - - - - - - - - - 5s. 3d. per Quarter.
Do. - - - & Writing - - - - 7. 6. per Do.
Do. - - or - - Do. - & Accompts ç 6. per Do.

Lancaſter, April, 1793.

* Aged 22.

Handbill for Edward Adlington's school, 1793. Interestingly his school was to be held in the old Concert Room or Theatre behind the Horse & Farrier Inn in Church St, vacant since the building of the new subscription theatre in St Leonardgate.

Soulby Collection, Cumbria Record Office, Barrow-in-Furness

CHAPTER EIGHT

Working Life

Life in service

The urban Georgian household ran on servants. In wealthier households the proportion of servants to family members might be in the order of four to one, but that proportion rapidly decreased further down the social scale. Most servants were women, and a high proportion of women were employed as servants. Men servants were a mark of status and the less they had to do, the higher the employer's ranking. Women acted as cooks, kitchen maids and housemaids. A small elite went on to be housekeepers or ladies' maids: the former were responsible for the management of the household especially where their employer was a bachelor; the latter shared in all aspects of their mistresses' lives and were expected to be on hand at all times. Men servants were much rarer in middle-class homes in Georgian times and usually acted as coachmen or gardeners. Merchants and tradesmen might have their apprentices or journeymen (paid employees) living with them, occupying a position half-way between master and servant. A certain number of servants in town-centre houses may have 'lived out' and this is certainly true of specialists like washer-women, who were called in periodically as washing accumulated.

We know that in London black boy servants were very fashionable in the early eighteenth century, but how widespread the fashion was outside the capital we do not know. By the mid- to late eighteenth century the naming of black servants had become mainstream; unless their colour is specifically stated we simply could not pick them out from the records, as in the case of John Dixon and Frances Johnson, described above.

Women servants lived in the house, but the men might well live over the coach-house or stables. On the whole their relationship with their employers was very different to that of their Victorian successors. They were closer, were not expected to be invisible, and were far fewer in number. When a Georgian talked of 'family' or 'friends' they were likely to mean the whole household, including servants. Quaker households, in particular, avoided great distinction between persons and maintained the old-fashioned close working relationship with their servants: the master working alongside his employees; the mistress spinning or sewing with her maids.

In Georgian Lancaster there was plenty of space for building at reasonable rates, so houses here tended to be quite spacious. In London or Bath they built tall narrow houses with attics and cellars adapted for servants. Frequently kitchens and stores were below ground level, in poorly-lit 'areas', protected from street level by railings. In Lancaster, by contrast, services tended to be concentrated in service wings at the rear of the house, with kitchens at ground level and servants' rooms above. Maidservants' beds might also occupy the undivided roof space. A number of good examples survive or have been recorded, such as those at 11 Chapel Street or at 80 Church Street. Occasionally there were separate servants' stairs in the service wing to avoid servants using the main stairs and perhaps carrying full chamber pots past unsuspecting guests! On the whole this was rare in Lancaster. More common was the reduction in quality of the staircase as it went up, with turned balusters and carved strings at 'family' levels, giving way to plain pine and simple mouldings by the servants' floor. In general the attitude to servants was closer and friendlier than was to be the case in the next century, when the 'green baize door' and separate stairs created a gulf between the two.

Servants were usually drawn from the countryside. Girls as young as thirteen or fourteen could go into service. It was considered a step up. At home they might be treated as unproductive, but if they sent part of their wages home their standing within their own family would rise. They would associate with employers of a higher social class and would learn polite manners which would help them if they married or set up shop later. Employers would hand down clothing or furnishings that were no longer fashionable to their servants, who would often pass them straight on to their mothers or younger sisters. Wages were very low, perhaps £5 a year for women servants, but the job was fairly secure and they received food and shelter free. In return they worked long hours with little time to call their own. This was not considered a problem at the time; for most people life was work and work was life. Men servants commanded a higher wage, but there were fewer of them and they often had specialised skills, such as horsemanship or husbandry.

Cooking was carried out over a range. Such ranges were a combination of open fire and separate cooking ovens and water boilers. In Georgian Lancaster the open fire element was still quite large and included the traditional crane and reckon hooks for cooking with a suspended pot or a 'yetling', a flat pan. As time went on the enclosed elements became more important and ornate. A good example of a Georgian cooking-range survived until recently at 4 Dalton Square, having been cast at the Halton foundry. Food among the

The basement kitchen of number 4 Dalton Square, which survived almost untouched until the 1990s. The house, inserted between two existing ones in about 1824, is unusual in Lancaster in having such services at cellar level, perhaps because of the relatively small size of the building plot. Most houses contained a ground-floor kitchen in a rear service wing. The semi-range with a crane for pots and a separate boiler was cast at the Halton Foundry, and is now preserved in Lancaster City Museum.

better-off households would include a much higher proportion of meat than we are accustomed to. A roast or boiled joint, as well as fish and perhaps chicken could be served up for even family meals, while entertainment of guests could involve a great many dishes, served simultaneously or in at most two courses, in the 'English manner'.

Kitchens also contained a water supply, often the only one in the house, with a large lead storage tank and a tap, and a slopstone or shallow sink for washing dishes in. The kitchen usually opened on to a yard where there was a well and pump.

Laundry of middle-class households was usually washed every five weeks, by the servants and by women who came in specially, to earn a little extra for their families. These might wash it on the spot or take it home. Washing was hung to dry on thorn hedges and on well-established 'drying grounds' on the fringes of the town, although here it might be vulnerable to theft. In Victorian times a disproportionately large number of Lancaster's washer-women lived at Golgotha, on the edge of the Moor. Here they had open ground and strong westerly winds, ideal for drying. One suspects that this arrangement may go back a long time. The infrequent washing of clothes meant that people did not change them as often as we do, and furthermore they needed multiples of each item to last them out.

Servants

Georgian towns ran on servants, whose employment ran a long way down the social scale. It is impossible to understand how houses worked without such cheap labour. Most servants in Lancaster would be women, as the majority of houses employing them were of the middling sort, unlike the gentry and nobility whose status was often counted in the number and gorgeousness of their footmen.

Service was seen as a good job, not yet as servile, and it was a way in which girls from poorer families could see a little of the world, learn polite manners and household management, and eventually perhaps marry and run their own shop or inn. Wages seem pitiful, as does the amount of spare time granted, but attitudes were different and the most important thing was 'keep', the guarantee of good and regular meals and access to medical attention.

Kitchens were labour-intensive, with all the food-preparation, cooking over an open fire or a simple range, and washing-up. There was also the perennial need for drawing water from the well, and the periodic washing of the family's clothes. Servants lived in attics, while unlike many larger towns Lancaster had a tradition of ground-floor kitchens in a rear service-wing, rather than in dark basements.

The few men-servants included coachmen and gardeners, some of whom would not have lived on the premises. Many apprentices and unmarried journeymen employed in the small-scale manufactories occupied a position similar to servants, living in the shop or workshop and sharing meals with the family.

The coach house and stable to 1 Queen St survives fairly complete, although now in separate ownership from the house. Coach houses such as this often had a hayloft over the ground floor, and sometimes accommodation for the coachman, who was likely to be the house's only male servant.

left The attic space in 80 Church St which still shows traces of its occupation by the maidservants. The main roof trusses divide the space into three, one larger to the east and two smaller to the west. These two borrow light from the staircase by windows set in the partition. The staircase itself starts at the second floor and is much plainer than the main stairs. The maids probably slept two to a bed in these attic rooms.

Good inventories of kitchen equipment survive for 9 Chapel Street in 1803 and for 12 Castle Park in 1819.[47]

No. 9 Chapel Street

In the Kitchen – One oven, one grate, nigards and screw, one crane and crooks, one grate for ashes, one towel roller and box, all the shelves, cupboards, drawers and dressers, one stone trough and lead pipes, one stove and back stone.

12 Castle Park

In the Kitchens. The oven, the range, the crane and crooks, the cinder grate, the small brass jack, the dresser and shelves, the oak cupboard between kitchens, the hot hearthplate and frontplate complete, the small iron boiler and grate, the brass boiler, grate and door, the wood frame and sliding doors over the boilers, the cupboard in passage.

Commercial and industrial life

The Georgian period was a time of great change in Lancaster's commercial life. At the beginning of the eighteenth century trade was very similar to what it had been in the Middle Ages, apart from the introduction of a few new trades such as that of peruke- (wig-) maker or tobacco-pipe maker. Trades were still very localised to particular streets, so that all ironmongers or tallow-chandlers, for instance, were grouped together in adjacent shops. The surviving system based on Freedom of the borough laid down rules as to who could and who could not practise a trade. Boys were usually apprenticed to a trade at the age of thirteen. Very few trades were open to women, although the parish might apprentice orphan girls as servants. Generally parents would try to set up their sons in a 'better' trade than their own, although it has to be said that there are many examples of sons following their fathers into the same trade. They would pay a sum of perhaps £40 to be apprenticed and in return would have their keep for the whole term of apprenticeship, usually seven years. In retail trades the apprentices, particularly the younger ones, would often live in the shop and be on call virtually all the time.

After completing their apprenticeship they were entitled to apply for the Freedom of the borough. With this they were entitled to practise a trade within the town. They also gained freedom from tolls here and in certain other towns and various other benefits, including the vote. It was customary to gain further experience as a journeyman (paid employee) for a couple of years but some former apprentices went straight into their own business. A successful trader might have two or three apprentices at a time, each at a different stage, and they would to a great extent teach each other the necessary skills, while the master himself might take the opportunity for more leisure. Both Apprentice Rolls and Freemen's Rolls are very useful in reconstructing the working population of the town. Both survive among the borough records.

Some traders were not Freemen. Among these were people who came to Lancaster for a purpose, like the stonemasons who worked on the Town Hall, Castle or Skerton Bridge, such as Robert Charnley or Joseph Muschamp, and did not expect to stay. Some were widows, whose husbands had carried on a trade. The widow might continue to run it until she could find a buyer or until her eldest apprentice could take over. A few women, mostly spinsters, ran millinery shops or small general shops to make a livelihood. Hat, bonnet and mantua-maker were typically female occupations. The 1818 trade directory lists no fewer than seven straw hat makers in Lancaster, all of them women. The popularity of split-straw weaving was perhaps a result of the wars with France – French prisoners-of-war seem to have introduced the art to this country. There is some evidence to suggest that women were moving into related occupations such as those of haberdasher and linen-draper by the end of the eighteenth century. As we have also seen, running a small school was also regarded as a respectable occupation for a lady.

Women were barred from becoming Freemen, while Quakers barred themselves by refusing to take an oath of allegiance. All of these paid an annual fine instead and appeared on the Stallenge ('stallholders') Roll. The latter records seems to be an exclusively Lancaster survival, although the practice almost certainly occurred widely. From 1685 to 1695 and from 1737 to 1795 there are continuous runs of these annual lists, which covered all the minor trades, such as clay tobacco-pipe makers, those carried out by Quakers or women, and a few others such as innkeeping, where turnover seems to have been very high. By comparing the Apprentice Rolls, the Freemen's Rolls and the Stallenge Rolls we can locate virtually everyone who traded in Lancaster in the eighteenth century. But we should not forget that there was a degree of avoidance; and a further group of unlicensed tradesmen is to be found in the Sessions books of the borough court, being fined for practising a trade without benefit of freedom or stallenge. Of course there was probably yet another group who simply got away with it, and of whom there is no record.

By the late eighteenth century this rigid system was starting to break down. Shops were no longer confined to same-trade streets. Trades could no longer be so easily defined. The Apprentice Rolls record a relatively few distinct trades at the beginning of the eighteenth century, such as butcher or barber, but by the end of the century many were calling themselves merchants and had their fingers in a great variety of pies. Besides, people were more mobile. It became irksome to be hedged around by so many restrictions when trade had become national or international. What had originally been intended to protect local traders now got in their way. Merchants increasingly purchased their Freedom, rather than obtaining it by apprenticeship. In Lancaster stallenge fines ceased in 1800, but Freemen and Apprentice Rolls carried on into the nineteenth century and the Freedom is still granted today, although it has long since ceased to have a practical purpose.

Most industries were on a very small scale until the very end of the period, when steam-powered textile mills began to creep into Lancaster, beginning at White Cross in 1802. The opening of the Lancaster Canal in 1797 meant that mills established along its banks could bring in coal and raw materials and take out the finished products by water. In practice cotton manufacture had little impact here until around 1820: Moor Lane Mills began about this time. Both Moor Lane main mill buildings survive, as does the oldest part of White Cross, and are fine and distinguished structures with good proportions and amazing multi-paned windows, with up to 81 panes per window. Undoubtedly the best of the mills have survived and are a benefit to Lancaster. What must have struck contemporaries was their size, particularly their height, when nothing else in the town went above three storeys. Other textile works, for silk, linen and sailcloth, were very small in scale and a number of manufactories were tucked away up yards rather than in purpose-built mills. When cotton finally made its impact on Lancaster its effect combined with that of a slump in overseas trade. Cotton began the transformation of the town into a principally working-class environment for the remainder of the nineteenth century. It also provided the first large-scale employment in a town which had previously consisted mostly of small businesses.

A delft-ware pottery on St George's Quay, established in 1745 and running probably until the 1780s, may have been a significant employer. Nine potters are listed by name in the Militia Ballot List of 1757[48] and, as this excluded men below 18 or above 50 years old, some older men and all the apprentices should be added to the workforce. The site of the pottery was long known as 'the Pothouses'. It was later used by John Brockbank as a shipyard, perhaps for building larger vessels.

Evidence survives patchily for some processes. Archaeology has revealed traces of dyeing or tanning on backland behind Church Street. Tanning was an extensive process involving water, bark storage barns and sequences of noisome pits in which hair was loosened and hides were gradually turned into leather. Because of the evil smell it usually occupied premises on the outskirts of the town. Two eighteenth-century tanneries in St Leonardgate are known from property deeds.[49] One was at the corner of Stonewell, the other at the north-eastern end of the street. Both were fed by streams which have now been culverted. The latter site shows a very typical urban sequence from open ground and orchards, to a tannery, to cottages and eventually to Victorian slum housing in a yard, mirroring the increasing density of population. A large pit found in the roadway of Chapel St, outside the tower of St John's church in about 1988, revealed huge numbers of cut sheep metapodial bones, typical evidence for extraction of neat's-foot oil, used in tanning lighter skins, such as those used for gloves.[50] The deposit clearly antedates the development of the area of Green Ayre for housing in the 1740s. Other occupations, such as that of tallow-chandler, were probably unpleasant neighbours, but preferable to tanners. The candle-house would contain large vats of hot tallow (animal fat), as well as wax for the most expensive candles. The most unpleasant residues undoubtedly came from the butchers' Shambles which from the 1770s ran back from the southern side of Market Street. Killing and butchering took place in the open and, without an effective drainage system, a horrible mess polluted the street.

Clay tobacco-pipes were manufactured up a yard in Penny Street by a succession of makers from about 1705. Like many other specialised items made in Lancaster, the trade with the West Indies must have accounted for a large proportion of products, and indeed, a single marked example of a pipe made by John Holland of Lancaster (d. 1754) was even found at the sunken pirate city of Port Royal in Jamaica.[51] A similar connection led to the building of a 'sugar-house' or sugar-refinery in St Leonardgate by Robert Lawson. Under various owners this survived for over a century. Research remains to be carried out on this, but there is evidence of at least two Germans from the

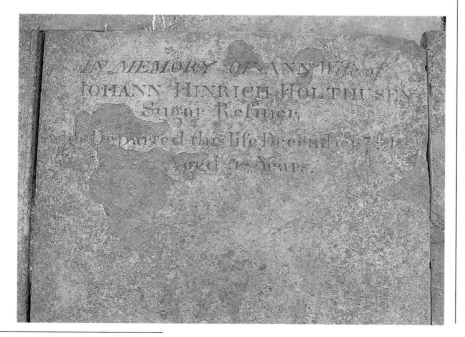

The tombstone of the wife Johann Hinrich Holthusen, Sugar Refiner, who died in 1824. Holthusen operated the sugar house in St Leonard-gate, and died some ten years later, but does not seem to be buried in Lancaster. Many Germans from Hanover were involved in this industry.

Hanover area working there, named Hinrich Holthusen and Heartwick Grippenhearl. The Hanover connection is noted in other British sugar-houses. Physical evidence survives in the form of long conical sugar-moulds of red earthenware, found on the site in 1929 when the Co-operative Society Garage was being built. Other moulds have since been found behind Church Street in excavations of 1988 and 1992 on Mitchell's Brewery site. Their findspot suggests that sugar loaves may have been supplied to grocers still in their moulds, or that the moulds were re-used for another purpose. The same distribution of sugar-moulds is noted in recent excavations in Chester.

Many smaller trades and industries were connected with shipping. Rope-walks were widespread, especially in St Leonardgate and by the old mill dam, wherever there was enough room for them. Anchor-smiths and sailcloth-weavers also plied a regular trade. Timber was stacked in all sorts of places, such as the Vicarage Fields and on Green Ayre, while there was a timber-pond on the Lune just upstream of Skerton Bridge. While local oak from as far away as High Furness was much used for shipbuilding in the early eighteenth century, demand quickly outstripped local supply. Edward Barrow in the 1720s and later John Brockbank travelled far and wide in search of timber.[52] Lancaster quickly became dependent upon Baltic fir and other softwoods for ships' planking and for house-carpentry.

Shops also changed over the course of the period. Nearly all were the retail outlets for manufactories within the town, and not purely for retail of goods made elsewhere, as is the case today. Tallow-chandlers, for example, made candles in a workshop but might have a shop on the street frontage in which to sell them. Cobblers and tailors made boots and clothes to order. There was virtually no demand – or supply – for ready-made items. Even grocers mixed, made up, or packaged raw materials. Only specialised items such as iron nails or pottery and glass were made elsewhere. Most purchases were made on credit, as shop-keepers knew their customers. Purchases were entered in a ledger and bills sent out at the end of the month or year. It was considered very odd to demand cash on the spot.

We know a great deal about the nature of shopkeeping in early Georgian Lancaster from the autobiography of William Stout. He had been through an apprenticeship to an ironmonger in the late seventeenth century, kept his own shop and moved on to mercantile and wholesale activities. Try as he might to shrug off the role of shopkeeper he kept coming back to it as his former apprentices failed in business or as he nursed a shop as an executor under a will or bankruptcy.[53] In his earlier days he often travelled to Sheffield to make contact with his suppliers; face-to-face contact was all-important in establishing trust for wholesale supply, especially in the absence of easy ways of paying remotely.

Shopping

Shops developed very considerably during the Georgian period. At the beginning of the eighteenth century most Lancaster shops would have been little different from their medieval predecessors, with a simple fold-down shutter which became a counter. By the later eighteenth century windows were mostly of glass, in small panes, often with a bow shape to maximise the amount of goods on display. In the early nineteenth century improvements in glass technology allowed much larger pieces to be made and, allied with improvements in lighting, enabled attractive window displays to entice customers to enter.

Most shops in the town were the retail front to a manufacture of some sort – clothes, shoes, chairs, candles etc. – often itself carried on up a yard behind. Even grocers and milliners, who dealt largely in goods made elsewhere, would package up and on occasions create their own wares.

Some specialised goods such as buttons or metal parts were already being made in places such as Birmingham and Clerkenwell in London, but a great proportion of everyday goods was still being made locally.

Many shopkeepers had their own warehouses to store surplus goods, while merchants used theirs to distribute bulk goods brought in by ship.

below In the 1790s Manchester was just embarking upon half a century of rapid growth as the entrepôt for all kinds of cotton goods. No wonder, then, that S. Patchet, draper, made a special trip there to stock her shop on Penny Street in 1793. It was usual in such handbills to emphasise the fashionable nature of the stock and the metropolitan or at least urban connections of the proprietor.

Soulby Collection, Cumbria Record Office, Barrow-in-Furness

S. PATCHET,

Penny Street Lancaster,

MOST GRATEFULLY ACKNOWLEDGES THE MANY FAVORS SHE HAS RECEIVED
From the Public in General ;
And Respectfully informs them, she is just returned from

MANCHESTER,

Where she has bought very low, a large and neat Assortment of
Printed CALICOES, MUSLINS, MUSLINETS and DIMITIES
from 16d per yard and upwards.

INDIA and BRITISH MUSLINS ⅞ wide; from 2s to 14s per yard.
MUSLIN Handkerchiefs and Yard wide MUSLINS from 14d to 10s.
Good choice of ¾ and Yard wide black MODES,
White and coloured PERSIONS, LACE, EDGING and RIBBONS,
IRISH and CUMBERLAND Ell-wide SHEETINGS &c. &c.
DROGHEDA, DOWLAS and DERRY CLOTH,
KENDAL CHECKS and STRIPES,
SHAWLS, SILK and Pocket HANDKERCHIEFS,
MEN and WOMAN'S STOCKINGS,
with many other ARTICLES
In the DRAPERY BUSINESS,
which will be sold on such TERMS
As she hopes will merit a continuation of the favors of her Customers.

Lancaster 30th March 1793.

H. Walmsley, Printer.

JAMES CHADWICK & Co.

TOBACCONISTS AND SNUFF

MANUFACTURERS,

BEHIND THE GENERAL COACH-OFFICE,

MARKET-STREET, LANCASTER;

Beg leave to acquaint their FRIENDS and the PUBLIC,

THAT THEY INTEND TO CARRY ON THE

Business in all its Branches,

And hope by strict ATTENTION and INDUSTRY
to recommend themselves to the
Patronage of the Public.

28th MAY, 1802.

H. Walmsley, Printer, New-Street, Lancaster.

left A handbill, printed by Walmsleys printers of Sun Street in 1802 for James Chadwick & Co., who combined the activities of tobacconist and the typically eighteenth-century trade of snuff manufacturing.

Lancaster Central Library

right Handbill issued in 1792 by Richard Dilworth, tallow-chandler, to counter rumours that he would be giving up business after ending his partnership with Thomas Noon. Tallow-chandlers made candles, the best ones from of wax, the cheaper ones from rendered beef fat (known as tallow). The candle-house where the tallow was boiled could be a rather noxious place.

Soulby Collection, Cumbria Record Office, Barrow-in-Furness

RICHARD DILWORTH,

TALLOW CHANDLER,

RETURNS HIS SINCERE THANKS TO HIS FRIENDS AND THE PUBLIC, FOR THEIR PAST FAVOURS,

AND RESPECTFULLY INFORMS THEM

That he continues the BUSINESS as USUAL in the BACK-LANE, LANCASTER,

WHERE THE FAVOURS OF THE PUBLIC WILL BE GRATEFULLY RECEIVED.

☞ On Account of a report which has been propogated, since he diffolved Copartnerfhip with Mr. Noon, that it was his intention to decline the Bufinefs; he thinks it a duty incumbent upon him to give this Information, eft his Cuftomers may be mifled by fuch Infinuations.

May 21ft, 1792.

ELIZABETH NOON,

MARKET-STREET, LANCASTER,

(Succeffor to Mrs. BONIS)

SENSIBLE of the candour and generous zeal with which the Ladies of Lancaster, and its vicinity, patronife thofe who endeavour to oblige, takes the earlieft opportunity of informing them, that fhe has taken Mrs. BONIS'S STOCK; and, for fome time paft, has been attentively employed in acquiring a knowledge of the STRAW HAT MANUFAC-TORY; which, with the affiftants engaged, who are proficient in the business, she intends to carry on, in the Shop lately occupied by Mr. DICKINSON, watch-maker, Market-street, adjoining her dwelling-house; and, by having a constant supply of the newest and most elegant patterns, flatters herself they will be found worthy the approbation of those who may please to favour her with their commands.

N. B. A good assortment of FUNERAL SILKS and BLACK CRAPES.

Nov. 10th, 1804.

Jackson's Print.

above Handbill for Elizabeth Noon, straw hat manufactory, 1804. Her business was in Market St and she later ran the Post Office in Market Square. She came from a long line of independent women, her grandmother, mother and sister all being innkeepers, the last at the Royal Oak Inn, Market Square.

Soulby Collection, Cumbria Record Office, Barrow-in-Furness

right Handbill for Thomas Frankland, grocer, 1791. His new business was in Pudding Lane, later known as Cheapside..

Soulby Collection, Cumbria Record Office, Barrow-in-Furness

THOˢ FRANKLAND

S THE LIBERTY OF INFORMING HIS FRIENDS AND THE PUBLIC,

hat he has opened a SHOP in PUDDING-LANE,

LANCASTER,

WHERE HE INTENDS CARRYING ON THE

ROCERY BUSINESS,

WHOLESALE AND RETAIL.

HE HAS LAID IN AN ASSORTMENT OF THE

FINEST FLAVOURED TEAS,

From the Eaft India Company's laft Sale;

ALSO,

REFINED and RAW SUGARS,

OF VARIOUS QUALITIES;

AND

LANCASHIRE & CHESHIRE CHEESE, &c.

WHICH HE INTENDS SELLING ON REASONABLE TERMS.

LANCASTER, November 12th 1791.

'Middle men' were starting to appear in many trades, but there was still a strong feeling that this was disreputable and unfair. Indeed, the practice was known as 'forestalling' and was seen as a means of taking an unfair profit from both supplier and buyer, and the Corporation had rules against it in the market.

The gentry would no doubt buy many of their clothes and much of their furniture and household ornaments in London, which was regarded as the centre for fashionable goods. However, most townsfolk had little opportunity, and little need, for shopping elsewhere. Lancaster was a sub-regional centre for north Lancashire, Furness, and south Westmorland, and events such as the Assizes and Race Week must have given a considerable benefit to local shops.

I brought down with me from London to Sheffeild about twenty pounds, which I laid out there in Sheffeild and Birmingham manufactories and got wel home the end of that weeke. [1688]

'In the 6ᵗʰ month this year I went with Richard Green to Liverpoole, where we bought in betwixt 2 and 300L worth of tobacco, most of it [in] bulke ... [1695]

Although both these references come from early in Stout's career it is clear that contacts were of long-standing benefit to him.

At the beginning of the eighteenth century the majority of Lancaster shops were of the medieval type, with a large opening protected at night by a shutter. This would be let down by day to form a counter. As glass became cheaper and oil lighting more reliable large shop windows became popular. They were only allowed a limited projection into the street so multi-paned and shallow-bowed windows were common. At the very end of the Georgian period the invention of plate glass and better lighting made possible very large display windows of the kind still used today.

We also know a great deal about shops at this period from handbills and advertisements put out by shopkeepers anxious to promote business or announce their takeover of an existing shop. The local newspaper, the *Lancaster Gazette*, is a useful source, while for handbills the Central Library Scrapbooks offer some but the Soulby Collection at Barrow-in-Furness is a tremendous resource. These all reveal essentially what the shopkeeper wished to be revealed.

Good descriptions of the reality of shops, as opposed to the way the shop-keepers portrayed themselves – the scatter of stock throughout the house and the general untidiness – can be gained from the Borough Court Rule Book. A few examples must suffice. Thomas Benn (28 July 1785) had a shop with bow window. James Harden's (22 March 1798) had boots, shoes, 250 lasts and leather, stockings, handkerchiefs and a shoemaker's seat. In the shop of James Raine (7 January 1802) were 2 warerooms, counting house and warehouse. In them he had a weight beam and scales, weights, general grocery stock, meal, cheeses, sugar, soap, candles, barrels of herring etc., and a handcart and truck.

John Nightingale's stock (7 February 1805) included 10 children's chairs, 6 armchairs, 22 rush bottomed chairs, six shuttles & two pairs of 'geers' (presumably some of the specialised tools of the trade). In his workshop were two lathes, a set of tools, a quantity of unfinished chairs, and ash & eller poles. William Steel, Christopher Johnson & James Steel (18 August 1808) were in partnership. They had three counters with mahogany tops, two writing desks, shelves and fixtures and a large stock of millinery, buttons etc. In the shop of John Bond (22 April 1813) were a great many cloth pieces and waistcoat pieces, buttons and button moulds, the shop counter, two pairs of scales and 10 weights.

Edmund Brevins (28 January 1819) had a shopboard (presumably the counter) and a stock of fabrics including fustian, velveteen, jean etc. while James Livingston (11 May 1820) had lengths of cloth, stockings, waistcoat pieces, hats, paper, a tea canister, beam and scales, weights (56, 28, 7 lbs), 17 gross of blackjacks (usually the word for a leather drinking vessel, but perhaps here some sort of button?) 17 gross of coat molds (buttons), 80 gross of small ditto, counter, desk and shelves. A shoemaker called Dickinson (19 April 1821) had three shoemakers' seats, 170 lasts, three boot trees, four pairs of 'sattan' shoes, one pair of 'sattan' boots, buttons, linings, leather, buckles, silk, 67 pairs of women's shoes, 27 pairs of men's, 25 pairs of children's, one pair of men's top boots, three pairs of women's boots, linen, a counter and fixtures.[54]

At this period we are seeing the continued local production of chairs, shoes etc. but the growth of a specialised supply industry for small articles which could be easier made in the industrial environment of London or Birmingham.

Ho! For the life of a sailor

Because of Lancaster's geographical location, as well as its Atlantic trading tradition, many young men must have felt the attraction of a sailor's life. They would have seen merchant ships moored at St George's Quay and the exotic cargoes being unloaded. Equally glamorous must have seemed the mariners (as they called themselves), their pockets jingling with coins, determined to have a good time while ashore, and with strange tales of exotic places. Clark claims that up to a thousand of Lancaster's menfolk were at sea when the census was taken in 1801, so shipping was one of the largest employers of labour before the local rise of the textile industry.[55] There was certainly a large disproportion between men and women at that date – 3,999 of the former and 5,031 of the latter, although the number of women in domestic service may have affected this as well. By the early eighteenth century many young men were being formally apprenticed to mariners, presumably masters of vessels, such as Thomas Barrow, John Calvert or Edward Noble, and later on to merchants and shipowners such as Dodshon Foster or the Rawlinson brothers for service on a named ship.[56]

It was a highly skilled job to navigate a small sailing ship across the Atlantic, and no less an

Tombstone of Thomas Atkinson, 'Captain of the Ship Mildred of this Port who with the whole of his Crew perished in a storm in the Gulf of Florida AD 1800 Aged 29 Years'.

Ships & Shipbuilders

Despite the difficulty of navigating the occasionally treacherous, tidal river, Lancaster was a significant port throughout the eighteenth century. Much of the town's prosperity came from this source. Ship ownership was widespread, although much of the trade was controlled by a handful of merchants led by the Rawlinson family. Many others also benefited from the overseas trade, since many specialised or luxury goods had a high value in the colonies and plantations, which were focused on a few crops such as sugar or cotton.

There was a ship-building industry of sorts in Lancaster from about 1700 until the 1820s. Its early days are unclear, and Lancaster was only one of several places where Edward Barrow built ships (Sunderland and Lindeth in Warton were others). Demand was intermittent and average size was small. By the middle of the century two sites had become established, one on the Green Ayre slightly upstream from the Old Bridge, and one below the bridge on the opposite bank. The first yard belonged to the Brockbank family. They were building from at least the mid-century and by 1817, when they launched their last ship, they had built

Tombstone of William Ashburner, Sailmaker, who died in 1791, aged 27. Sailcloth was produced in small workshops at this time, wherever looms could be fitted in. Each ship would also carry skilled sailmakers who could mend and maintain the large stock of sails required.

left A detail of a watercolour drawing by Gideon Yates of Lancaster from the Ridge, 1811. A ship is on the stocks at Brockbank's shipyard which is enclosed by a wall on the Green Ayre, just next to the Georgian houses on Cable Street. Three vessels are tied up on the Quay, while another is just upstream.

Lancaster City Museums

A painting attributed to John Emery, showing Brockbank's shipyard. The ship's figurehead of Admiral Lord Nelson identifies it as *Trafalgar*, a ship of 267 tons built in 1806 for service in the 'Guinea trade' (i.e. slaving) and registered in Liverpool by the Hinde brothers, Lancaster merchants who had moved their base there. In the background are the warehouses on St George's Quay and the remains of the Old Bridge. To the left, a small vessel is being caulked with hot pitch, while a pair of timber wheels for moving large logs lie at the centre.

Lancaster City Museums

in excess of 130 vessels. The site of their yard is now marked by Sainsbury's supermarket. On occasions they built larger vessels elsewhere, such as downstream at the Pothouse, where David Cragg saw *Clarendon* launched in 1792. Until 1802 they were hampered by the position of the Old Bridge downstream of the yard, which meant all ships had to be launched 'light', and floated through the arches before masts and yards could be added. The other yard changed hands several times, the owners including James Smith, followed by his widow, then Worthington & Ashburner. It was not as prolific as Brockbanks. Ships grew rapidly in size during the later eighteenth century, and Lancaster could not keep up in the end, as ships of 300–400 tons were generally as large as the river would take before substantial changes to its course in the nineteenth century.

Oak was the timber of desire in the early eighteenth century, and local shipbuilders travelled far and wide in the remaining woods of Furness and the Lake District and as far afield as Shropshire and North Wales in search of suitable supplies. Soon, however, trees of appropriate size were unavailable, and the industry used imported Baltic pine, available in huge quantities and fetched in special ships.

Lancaster also produced sailcloth, fittings, anchors, ropes etc., and no doubt the supplying of provisions for long voyages kept many bakers and butchers in business.

achievement to bring it successfully up the twisting river Lune to port at the end of its voyage. It was a risky business and the attrition in small ships was huge, especially in the periods of stormy weather which periodically racked the coast. It was very difficult to get a sailing ship off a lee shore if a storm blew up suddenly. There was a constant turnover of skilled seamen and opportunities for command came early to those who showed promise. Successful masters usually became part-owners, and could retire from the sea as a shipowner. It was normal to divide ships into shares of 1/64, so an individual might have shares in several ships, thus spreading the risk of loss should any particular ship be lost at sea. Shares of 1/64 might be grouped together, and could be sold or inherited. An example of this can be seen in the will of James Moore, 1810,[57] where he left 1/8 share in the ship *James* of Lancaster to his daughter Eleanor Ross, as well as 1/8 share in the ship *Aid* of Lancaster, 1/16 share in the *Pusey Hall* of Lancaster and 1/8 share in a new ship 'now building at Whitby in the County of York' to his son Thomas Moore and executors. (Whitby was a notable shipbuilding port at this time.)

Tombstone of John Tomlinson, mariner, who died in 1801.

Wooden ships with hemp rigging had a limited life. While some survived for a century, the majority had a realistic life of about a dozen years; some came to grief through shipwreck or capture, especially given the almost constant state of war in the eighteenth and early nineteenth centuries. Ships required constant maintenance, such as 'careening' to remove marine growth from the hull or re-rigging when the hemp ropes wore out. Ships spending any time in port would be 'rigged down', their topmasts and standing rigging being removed. Caulking and tarring to seal the ship's hull were also regular activities.

As we have seen, the sea provided an indirect living for many suppliers in Lancaster. Rope, sailcloth, timber and anchors were all in regular demand. There was also demand for a pool of casual labour. It was normal for mariners to sign up for a single voyage at a time, and crews were often made up to number at the last moment from quayside inns. Ships also had to be loaded and unloaded, requiring an irregular number of casual labourers. Ships attempted to come up river under sail if they could, but contrary winds and tides often meant that they had to be 'tracked' (i.e. pulled by rope) from the shore by men or horses, hauled by rowing skiffs, or even rowed using 'sweeps' (huge oars) over the side. 'Carmen' operated carts upon the quay, carrying goods to warehouses or elsewhere in the town. They operated much like modern taxis from a rank at the end of the quay, being used in a strict order of first come, first served. Their written regulations date only from 1830, but no doubt reflect earlier practice.[58]

Many mariners were single men, having few possessions and a roving lifestyle. When ashore they may have lived in inns or taken a room or two in a shared house. We can track down a few mariners and their widows in the records of the borough court through their ownership of distinctive possessions. These include conch shells, which were regarded as great curiosities, brought back from Pacific, and parrots. A parrot and cage seem to have been a very acceptable gift for a wife left at home. Examples of this are Dorothy Boulton, a widow, who had 4 'conk' shells and a parrot and cage in 1812[59] or Joseph Wilkinson who had 2 'conque' shells in 1815.[60]

The Borough Court Rule Book also lists the contents of what may be a typical mariner's house, that of William Greaves (8 March 1804). The contents of twelve named rooms are listed, including a Bible, an eight days clock with mahogany case, one ship (model?), a quantity of blocks and ropes, one ship buoy, and two oars etc.[61]

The Marine Society[62] was a self-help society which supported former masters and mates, while levies on mariners' pay, evidenced by the Seamen's Sixpence Register (1747–1851)[63] helped to provide a living for old or sick mariners, but many simply did not survive the rigours of the life. They succumbed to war, drowning, shipwreck, fever or simple over-exertion, since there were few mechanical aids to their labour.

Occasionally ships' masters survived all the perils of the sea and enjoyed life in retirement. Such men became respected for their experience and skill; a master mariner had to be able to deal with cargoes, finance and matters of life and death without any external support, and required qualities of independent judgement and maturity beyond those of most landsmen. Captain Thomas Greenwood received a present of a silver cup worth 100 guineas from the underwriters at Lloyds for having made no fewer than 32 successful voyages to the West Indies and having on one occasion fought off a French corvette.[64] Captain Walker, formerly in the West Indies trade, who lived in Castle Park, left a model warship to Thomas and Edward Hewitson in 1804[65] and this found its way to the Town Hall, where it was noticed in 1820.[66] It is still in the town's ownership, but nowadays can be seen at Lancaster Maritime Museum. Walker's obituary[67] states '... [he] was much attended to by the most ingenious builders, for his skill and knowledge in the art of shipbuilding'.

The resilience and resourcefulness of Lancaster's mariners must have given it a considerable advantage during the Georgian period, while the leaching away of such talent to Liverpool in the early nineteenth century no doubt contributed in part to the town's decline.

Social Life

CHAPTER NINE

High life

The relatively sudden increase in prosperity led to great changes in Lancaster. One way of celebrating the sudden accession to wealth was to build a new house, or to modernise an existing one. Two adjacent houses in Church St demonstrate the options. At number 76 Oliver Marton, a successful lawyer, acquired an old house in 1723 and refronted it in the latest style, decorating the interior to match. He then went on to ally his family to gentry families in the county by marriage, his elder son becoming MP for the town and his younger son its vicar. Next door, at modern numbers 78–80, Dr Daniel Wilson, a younger son of local gentry, whose family seat was at Dallam Tower, and himself a clergyman without benefice, pulled down the existing building and built a wholly new and fashionable house with a bow front on its site in 1772–75. That it stood on the site of ancient buildings in the Roman civil

A Roman altar to the god Mars Cocidius discovered in 1797 when the northern side of the Castle was extended. The powerful and the educated among Georgian society felt themselves to be very much the successors of Rome, with a mighty empire and a role to bring civilisation to the world. It was no mere fancy that dressed monumental effigies of eminent Georgians in togas or Roman armour. The finding of such an inscription must have given a sense of legitimacy to the civil powers which now occupied the ancient site.

left Numbers 78–80 Church St, built in 1772–75 for Dr Daniel Wilson, a large house typical of many belonging to minor gentry families, designed for entertaining. The windows in the gable end light the staircase and the servants' rooms (see page 50).

right Number 76 Church St, home of the Marton family from 1723. Oliver Marton refronted a much older house in the latest style and acquired a detached garden on the other side of the street where he built the Music Room, a grand summer-house with superb plasterwork by Swiss-Italian craftsmen.

settlement of Lancaster must have added an unexpected classical frisson to the project.[68]

For members of the merchant class there was no shame in trade and, unlike their Victorian successors who tried to move as far away from the source of their wealth as they could, Georgian merchants frequently lived and worked in the same place. They might have a grand house, but part of it would be the 'counting house' (in modern terms an office), often with a warehouse for goods adjoining it. There was no great cultural or geographical divide between home and work.

Even the country houses of the local gentry were not just symbols of power but also places where actual government and law administration took place. Anyone who had something to offer in exchange would seek out these powerful men for favours, employment or support. They also sat as magistrates upon all manner of civil cases. Houses were not just for living in; they were where business and politics were transacted. In which room of the house you were received was a mark of your social standing and expectations, and could range from the front hall to the bedchamber. Lancaster had seats of gentry of the middling sort, with few aristocrats. The Duke of Hamilton at Ashton Hall was the exception, coming from an old-established Scottish family, with its main house at Hamilton Palace.

Number 24 Castle Park, built in 1767 or just before by Mr Machell. Upon his untimely death, it was sold to Dr Thomas Wright. It is typical of the large comfortable houses enjoyed by middle-class professionals in the Georgian period.

A high proportion of the local gentry class was of relatively recent origin, often as the result of fortunes made from the law. The Fenwicks at Burrow, the Martons of Lancaster and Capernwray and the Benisons of Hornby all belonged to this category. Others, such as Col Charteris of Hornby Castle, had made their fortune by more questionable means such as gambling, although in his family's case, alliance with the Wemyss family had brought legitimacy, but did not save him and his wife from a rough handling by the townsfolk in 1745.

There were also several old Catholic gentry families in the area, such as the Cliffords of Quernmore Park or the Daltons of Thurnham. Recusancy (refusal by Catholics to attend the mandatory Protestant church services) had usually led to poverty, of a relative kind, due to the fines imposed on royalists and recusants in the previous century, but one should not underestimate their local influence.

It was not only the minor gentry with town houses and new merchant classes that were to be found in Georgian Lancaster. There were also clergymen, doctors, surgeons and lawyers, forming a sort of educated and professional elite. Such people usually had a wider perspective of the world than their fellow-townsfolk; they might have been to one of the universities (though the education served up at Oxford and Cambridge in Georgian times was often quite bizarre) and they would have contacts with fellow professionals in other towns and cities, including Liverpool and London.

The gentry for their part acted as magistrates, served as MPs and as naval and military officers, usually buying their commissions. Because the first-born son generally inherited a family's wealth, younger sons tended to make up much of the clergy, particularly the upper clergy. Before the creation of the county councils in the late nineteenth century much of the administration of the region fell upon them as magistrates or through service on the Grand Jury. Of course they had a particular point of view and favoured their own class, particularly in matters of riot or preservation of game, both of which became major issues in the troubled years after Waterloo.

All these groups tended to meet socially during the period of the two Assizes and during the week of race meetings usually held in June. Then there would be a flurry of assemblies, balls, card-parties, entertainments and plays at the theatre, with the associated match-making and intrigue that we see in novels of the period, such as those of Jane Austen. Georgian houses in

The Assembly Room in King St, built in 1759. Built to accommodate social gatherings, this Assembly Room had two floors with separate access so that two functions could proceed simultaneously. Profits from its letting helped to support Penny's Hospital, a set of twelve almshouses next door, built in 1720.

Penny's Hospital, built as almshouses in 1720 under the will of Alderman William Penny and still serving its original purpose. The design is notably old-fashioned and harks back to the seventeenth century. The Assembly Room (see page 67) was built to raise funds for Penny's Hospital, which is now run by Lancaster United Charities.

The Judge's Lodging, which stands on a very ancient site, was built in 1639 as the town house of Thomas Covell, Governor of Lancaster Castle. In the eighteenth century its windows were converted to sashes. In 1824 it became the lodging for the Circuit Judges when they came for the Assizes, and in the 1970s it became a museum.

Lancaster frequently show evidence of their social uses in having large reception rooms or suites of rooms which could be thrown together by opening up screens.[69]

High life and low life sometimes came together. Race-meetings held on the Marsh from about 1758 until 1797 and then on the Moor from 1809 attracted a wide audience ranging from the gentry who admired horseflesh, and enjoyed gambling, down to the touts and pickpockets who infested the crowds. Drink flowed liberally at such gatherings and they were a source of concern to the magistrates, involved in maintaining law and order. During the race-week cock-fights would also take place. A 'main' of cocks consisted of thirteen pairs of birds, fitted with metal spurs, pitted against each other in succession, with gambling upon the results. These fights took place in a circular arena, sometimes roofed and sometimes open to the elements, with seats for the spectators around the edge. In 1765 such a match took place in Skerton, while the Moor was the location for a match in 1774. From 1775 cock-fights took place at the new cockpit in Back Lane (King Street) but by 1802 this was in use as an extension of the market. Public opinion was moving against such cruel sports by then. Again both high life and low life combined in these essentially male activities.

Female activities, by contrast, were heavily circumscribed and there could be little mixing of social classes except by way of charity. Visits and tea-drinkings were a common feature of female activity for the leisured classes. Tea and coffee, rare at the beginning of the eighteenth century, were still expensive and involved a highly formalised social ritual. Charity was another opportunity for socialising. It was felt to be a particularly female attribute and apart from individual acts of charity like visiting the sick and relieving the poor there were many organisations such as 'lying-in societies' which provided baby clothes for poor women. Towards the end of the century arose the Dispensary movement, which was a fore-runner of the hospital system and brought health care to poorer people who previously had nothing.[70] Subscribers to the Dispensary were able to distribute tickets to deserving cases, bringing with it a web of patronage.

Promenading was popular with both sexes, and was an opportunity for informal conversation, courting and display of new fashions, rather like the Italian *passeggiata*. In the early part of the century Green Ayre was popular for evening strolls, but from at least the late 1770s a new walk was available in the form of 'Ladies Walk', which ran upriver roughly from where Skerton Bridge was later to stand. It is shown on Binns' map of Lancaster 1821 as a long straight walk bordered by trees, having a drainage dyke on one side and the old medieval mill-dam on the other, and running parallel to the river. It was similar to a number of other contemporary urban promenades such as

Lancaster Races

The earliest race-meetings were held, perhaps semi-legally, on an island known as Salt Ayre in the middle of the river in the early eighteenth century. More overt racing took place on the Marsh from about 1758 until 1797. It fell into abeyance for a few years until a new course was opened on the Moor in 1809, the site being now roughly bisected by the M6 motorway. The attraction of racing was undoubtedly the pitting of horse against horse, at a time when a gentleman's accomplishments included judgement of horses, riding and breeding. But gambling also attracted a rougher element, while race-meetings also traditionally included side-shows, and drinking-booths.

The new race-course of 1809 lay half inside and half outside the borough boundary, which led to a problem of jurisdiction. Picking of pockets, and stealing of pocket-books and watches was commonplace. The borough constable, and later the Watch, were unable to apprehend criminals who acted outside the borough. Later still the jurisdiction problem caused a farcical situation between the borough and the county police.

The race-meetings were another occasion when gentry came into town, and race week was generally a good week for the theatre. A less genteel pursuit associated with the races was the holding of a 'Main of Cocks', between the gentlemen of one county and another. This, too, introduced a rougher element into the town.

below Until 1797 Lancaster Races were held upon the Marsh to the west of the town, as indicated by this detail from Yates's map of Lancashire, 1786. At an earlier stage the island of Salt Ayre in the river Lune had been used. It can be seen just north of the racecourse.

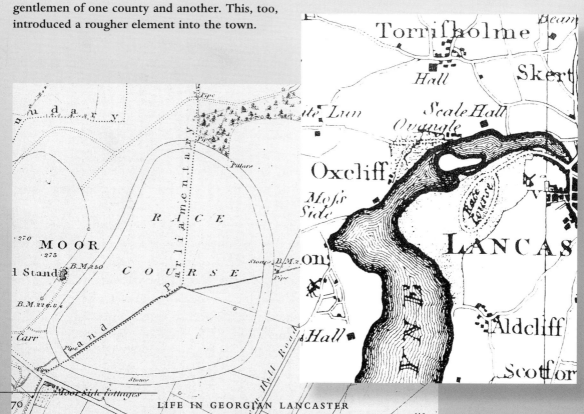

LANCASTER RACES, 1809,

ON TUESDAY the 27th of June, A PLATE OF FIFTY POUNDS, given by JOHN DENT and PETER PATTEN, Esquires, Members for the Borough, for Three and Four Years Olds. Three years old to carry 6st. 8lb. and four years old 8st. 4lb. Fillies allowed 3lb. The best of three two-mile heats. — 2 2 / 1 1

Duke of Hamilton's b. c. Peter Little, 4 years old, Benjamin Smith, black. W. N. W. Hewitt Esq's b. c. M'George, by St. George, 4 years old, John Johnson, white.

On WEDNESDAY the 28th THE TOWN'S PLATE OF FIFTY POUNDS, for Horses that never won £50 at one time, Matches and Sweepstakes excepted. The best of three three-mile heats. Three years old to carry a feather, four years old, 7st. 6lb. five years old, 8st. 6lb. six years old, 8st. 9lb. and aged horses, 8st. 12lb. Mares and Fillies to be allowed 3lb.

Mr. Uppelby's b. f. by Shuttle, 3 years old, James Raynor, yellow, & black cap. W. N. W. Hewitt. Esq's b. c. Stilton, by Stamford, 4 years old, John Johnson, white.

Mr. Coulson's ch. c. by Expectation, 4 years old, John Gray, white, & black cap.

On THURSDAY the 29th, the NOBLEMEN and GENTLEMEN'S SUB-SCRIPTION PLATE of SEVENTY POUNDS, for all ages. The best of three three-mile heats. Three years old to carry a feather, four years old. 7st. 4lb. five years old, 8st. 4lb. six years old 9st. and aged horses 9st. 4lb Mares and fillies to be allowed 3lb. A winner of one plate of £50 or upwards, in the present year, to carry 3lb. extra. of two 5lb. and of three or more, 8lb.

Duke of Hamilton's b. c. Peter Little, 4 years old, W. Clark, black. W. N. W. Hewitt Esq's b. c. Stilton, by Stamford, 4 years old, John Johnson, white.

LORD ARCHIBALD HAMILTON, } Stewards.
AND
JOHN DALTON, Esq. Jun.

All disputes to be determined by the Stewards, and their determination to be final.

To start each Day at 1 o'Clock.

§ All Dogs found on the Race-Ground will be destroyed.

Ordinaries—At the King's Arms on Tuesday and Thursday; and at the Royal-Oak, on Wednesday.

Mr. Stanton's Company of Comedians will perform every night during the Races.

... Moss, Lancaster)

TO BE FOUGHT,

BY WAY OF A LONG MAIN,

At the House of Mr. JAMES SANDERS, the Sign of the GREEN DRAGON, in
GALGATE.

On Monday next the 7th of July, Instant.

FORSHAW	lb.	oz.	JENKINSON	lb.	oz.
Alexander	3	8	Hentall	3	4½
Dr. Martin	3	12	Holler	3	13
Bother 'em	3	13½	Beau Greave	3	13
J. Duke of Richmond	3	14½	Wonder	3	13½
F. Alice	4		Bogart	4	
F. Ready & Willing	4	3½	Pilling Moss	4	
J. Tarn Water	4	4	Tickle 'em Billy	4	1
F. Dub Skelper	4	5	John Sail	4	5
F. Useful Cub	4	5½	Chips and Shavings	4	5
F. Great Ruth	4	5½	F. Scotforth Frolic	4	5½
F. Limellong-rock	4	6½	F. John Cragg	4	7
F. Sir Peter	4	6½	J. John Blackburn	4	8
F. Idle Jack	4	9	F. Duke of York	4	15

Leicester's 'New Walk', Tunbridge Wells' 'The Pantiles' and York's 'New Walk' by the river Ouse.[71]

A contemporary description comes from John Harden, an Irish artist who settled in the Lake District. In September 1798[72] he and his party promenaded this way in an evening, in just the approved manner, along:

> ... the Lady's walk, a niceley [sic] planted stretch along the river above 1 mile & ½ very beautiful, so to the Aquaduct a splendid work ...

Despite the presentment of the Mayor and Bailiffs in 1808 at the Borough Court for failing to repair the walk at Ladies Walk it survived until 1916–17, when it was demolished by German POWs to make the new roadway of Kingsway (Caton Road).

Even more fashionable pastimes were occasionally seen. The velocipede, or hobby-horse, a rather ungainly primitive bicycle without pedals, paddled along by its user, was invented in 1819 and had a brief vogue in fashionable London society. As early as 1822 a local man named Atkinson had a velocipede among his personal goods, being distrained upon by the Borough Court![73] What a Corinthian he must have seemed in provincial Lancaster society!

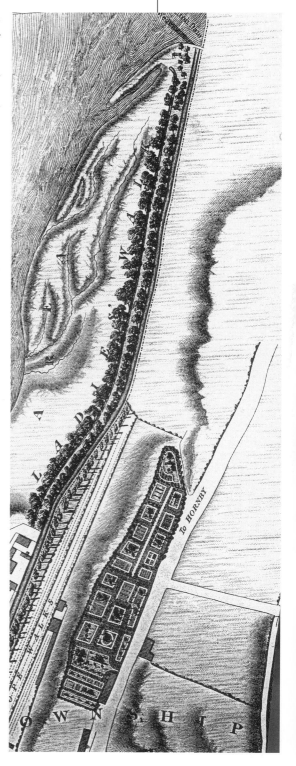

Ladies' Walk, Lancaster's fashionable riverside promenade, from Binns' map of 1821. The promenade finally disappeared under the new Caton Road in 1916. The walk ran parallel to the river and started at the Bridge Houses (just visible bottom left), running up to the ancient Dalton Dam at the top, where the Lune ceased to be tidal. It ran between trees and was a place for evening promenades in fashionable clothes, to see and be seen. The 'Ladies' of Ladies' Walk were the nuns of Syon Abbey, Middlesex, who had owned the land in the Middle Ages.

    LIFE IN GEORGIAN LANCASTER

Street life

Before the eighteenth century anyone venturing out at night did so at their peril: partly it was the danger of being robbed and murdered, but mostly of falling down holes or over obstructions in the dark streets. The first move to banish this was the installation of streetlights. When they first appeared in Lancaster is unknown, but the presentation of the Bailiffs in 1740 at the Borough Court for not lighting the lamps suggests that they were already in existence.[74]

Regular accounts for these oil lamps appear in the 1770s onwards with items such as; '£51 14s. 7½d. for oil, candles, lighting & repairing the Lamps'.[75] That they may only have been seasonal is suggested by the 1797 resolution[76] 'that bailiffs light the lamps for the ensuing winter'. In 1803 a reward of 10 guineas was offered for conviction of those breaking glass lamps in the borough.[77] An interesting survival is a handbill, 'The Lamplighter's Address', of 25 December 1817, containing verses printed to extract a 'Christmas Box' from the towns-people.[78] A contract for lighting the town in 1812 specified 169 oil lamps.[79] By 1817 the Corporation had ceased to pay for lamps and had pushed the cost on to householders, perhaps as a result of falling revenues.[80]

The town was lit with gas for first time in February 1827,[81] the gas coming from the new corporation gasworks on St George's Quay. It must have seemed the dawning of a new age.

Sedan chairs were popular and enabled ladies to be carried to balls and theatre performances without dirtying their shoes or getting wet. Although their use was widespread in Georgian towns the evidence for use in Lancaster is not easy to find. A handbill advertising rules for the New Chairmen (Clapham of Penny Street and Cock of Bridge Lane) survives[82] and implies that there were, or had been, others employed in this line (the Old Chairmen?). This handbill implies that the Playhouse was a good source of trade, perhaps worth more than the usual sixpence.

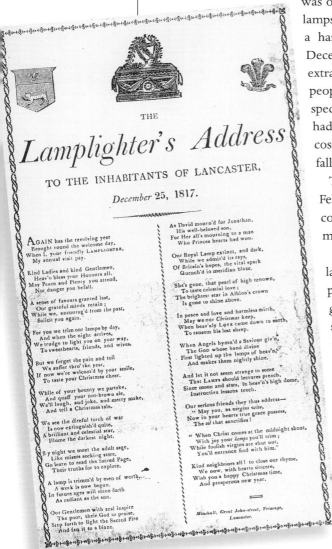

THE

Lamplighter's Address

TO THE INHABITANTS OF LANCASTER,

December 25, 1817.

AGAIN has the revolving year
Brought round the welcome day,
When I, your friendly LAMPLIGHTER,
My annual visit pay.

Kind Ladies and kind Gentlemen,
Heav'n bless your Honours all,
May Peace and Plenty you attend,
Nor danger you befall.

A sense of favours granted last,
Our grateful minds retain ;
While we, encourag'd from the past,
Solicit you again.

For you we trim our lamps by day,
And when the night arrives,
We trudge to light you on your way,
To sweethearts, friends, and wives.

But we forget the pain and toil
We suffer thro' the year,
If now we're welcom'd by your smile,
To taste your Christmas cheer.

While of your bounty we partake,
And quaff your nut-brown ale,
We'll laugh, and joke, and merry make,
And tell a Christmas tale.

We see the direful torch of war
Is now extinguish'd quite,
A brilliant and celestial star,
Illume the darkest night.

By night we meet the adult sage,
Like misers seeking store,
Go learn to read the Sacred Page,
Their truths for to explore.

A lamp is trimm'd by men of worth,
A work is now begun.
In future ages will shine forth
As radiant as the sun.

Our Gentlemen with zeal inspire
The poor, their God to praise,
Step forth to light the Sacred Fire
And fan it to a blaze.

As David mourn'd for Jonathan,
His well-beloved son,
For Her all's mourning to a man
Who Princes hearts had won.

Our Royal Lamp extinct, and dark,
While we admir'd its rays,
Of Britain's hopes, the vital spark
Quench'd in meridian blaze.

She's gone, that pearl of high renown,
To taste celestial love ;
The brightest star in Albion's crown
Is gone to shine above.

In peace and love and harmless mirth,
May we our Christmas keep,
When heav'nly Love came down to earth,
To ransom his lost sheep.

When Angels hymn'd a Saviour giv'n,
The God whose hand divine
First lighted up the lamps of heav'n,
And makes them nightly shine.

And let it not seem strange to some
That LAMPS should lectures preach,
Since moon and stars, in heav'n's high dome,
Instructive lessons teach.

Our serious friends they thus address—
" May you, as *virgins wise*,
Now in your hearts true grace possess,
The *oil* that sanctifies !

" When Christ comes at the midnight shout,
With joy your *lamps* you'll trim ;
While foolish virgins are shut out,
You'll entrance find with him."

Kind neighbours all ! to close our rhyme,
We now, with hearts sincere,
Wish you a happy Christmas time,
And prosperous new year.

Minshull, Great John-street, Friarage,
Lancaster.

The streets were kept clean by two forces – prosecution of those who left rubbish in front of their doors, and a financial incentive to recycle rubbish. We cannot be sure how effective the first was – there is a monotonous catalogue of offenders in the various borough court sessions books. The incentive to recycle may have worked better, because some rubbish, especially horse dung, had a value as manure. Sweepers known as 'scavengers' gathered such materials and indeed paid a 'farm' or a small fee to the Bailiffs for the privilege. According to the *Lonsdale Magazine* of 1820,[83]

> ... the streets are kept exceedingly clean, on account of the poor being allowed to collect the dirt; by which some poor families are almost maintained, who would otherwise burthen [i.e. be a burden to] the parish.

It is clear that many small craftsmen and manufacturers regarded the street in front of their premises as an extension of their workshops, and often left finished wares, waste or carts loaded with goods standing there for long periods. This may not have mattered much in the early eighteenth century, but increasing traffic made it more dangerous. By the end of the century presentments in the Borough Court show that speeding was already becoming a menace. In 1802 the driver of the Liverpool coach was presented for 'furious driving' in Penny Street,[84] while the Dragoons quartered here were also accused of riding through the streets at full gallop, which must have been frightening for pedestrians and onlookers.[85]

In a small town like Lancaster it must have been difficult for 'respectable' men to visit brothels discreetly. Probably they waited for trips to the

left Handbill for the 'New Chairmen', early nineteenth century. Their name suggests that there were some existing chairmen who operated sedan chairs within the town. Most of their business must have been done during the Assizes, and the Race week when the theatre was also busy.
Lancaster Central Library

This handbill is actually the only direct evidence we currently have for the use of sedan chairs in Lancaster. The light-hearted sport of sedan chair racing (*right*), pioneered by Lancaster's Georgian Festivals, gives a real insight into the practicalities and difficulties of the task.

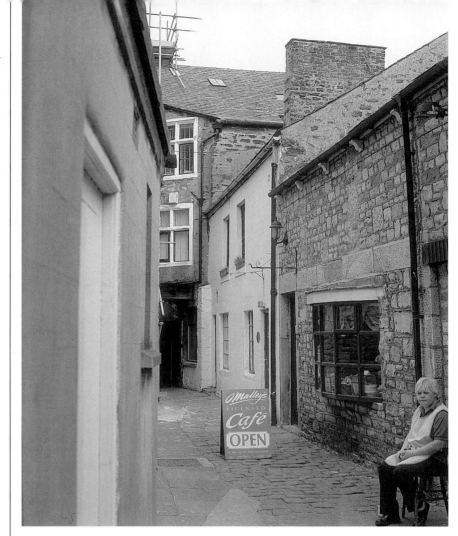

A modern view of Bashful Alley, which provides a short cut between Market St and King St. In the eighteenth century it was known as 'Swap Cunte Alley', presumably on account of its use by prostitutes.

metropolis to satisfy their appetites. The 'houses of ill-repute' or 'disorderly houses', of which we do hear, no doubt served the sailors and other transients, who did not care too much for their reputation. Their known locations on St George's Quay[86] and in Bridge Lane[87] reflect the traditional poorest roughest area of the town in later, Victorian, times. We hear of prosecutions such as those of Eliz Simpkin, Elizabeth Marshal and Margaret Heaton (alias 'Kendale Pegg') for acting as procuresses and owners of disorderly houses in the 1760s.[88] However, there is some evidence for more passing liaisons, probably involving an even lower class of whore. The alley linking Market Street and King Street, now known as 'Bashful Alley', appears from the borough records[89] to have been called 'Swap Cunte Alley' for much of the eighteenth century. 'Swap' in this case does not mean 'exchange' but is an old dialect word for any cash or barter transaction.[90] In any case the meaning is quite clear.

The office of Bellman was instituted in the seventeenth century or even earlier. The Bellman had important role in spreading news and making official proclamations at a time before Lancaster had its own newspaper – the *Lancaster Gazetteer* (later *Gazette*) did not appear until 1801, although *Gore's Liverpool Advertiser* and *The Cumberland Pacquet* provided Lancaster with some local news. The Bellman had a regular route around the town, his thirty-two stopping points chosen for their crowded nature and good acoustics. Wherever he stopped he would ring his bell to gather attention and then deliver his news, proclamation or advertisement. His stopping places were listed in detail on 16 November 1773.[91] Here are a few:

1st   At the corner of the Town Hall facing New Street

2   China Lane End

3   Meeting House Lane End facing Mr Recorder Fenton's House

4   Upon the Castle Hill facing Mr Richard Salisbury's House

5   At the corner of Mrs Alice Taylor's House leading to the Castle Gates

6   Upon the Rampart opposite the Alms Houses

... ending with

32   In the Market Street at the Fish Stones

Many kinds of goods were sold by street hawkers. Some of those who paid the stallenge were regulars at market; chapmen, pedlars, market women with butter and cheese etc. The Rule Book gives examples of men with carts whose stock-in-trade was butter and eggs, like John Ayrey (1786) or William Stockdale (1804).[92] In all probability there were milk-sellers, knife-grinders and others so familiar from the sets of engraved London street cries. This sort of market was positively protected by periodic notices warning against 'forestalling' or buying up of goods by middlemen. Cattle and sheep would be a common sight in the street as they were brought to market or led through by Scottish drovers on the long road to London. The intimate relationship between towns and agriculture had not yet been broken. Many freemen kept cattle on the Marsh, until its enclosure and regulation in 1796, while on the evidence of the Rule Book, pigs frequently occupied back yards even in the town centre, such as those of John Nightingale, chair-bodger (1805)[93] and John Jackson, victualler (1806).[94]

Privies were usually situated in yards and gardens in Lancaster. In larger cities 'nightsoil' men called after dark to clear the cesspits. Some nightsoilmen used special tank carts or large two-handled covered tubs to carry away the contents. What practice was employed in Lancaster is unknown, but at 20 Castle Park, which retains a quite remarkable privy house,[95] access for clearance was provided at a lower level, via the coach house, so that it did not involve bringing the noisome contents through the house.

Night life

For working people the day started early in Georgian times. Farm work began at dawn, while masons and carpenters would be at work by 6 a.m., often after a longish walk. At the other end of the scale a growing number of people did not have to work at all; their income came from the proceeds of land, industry or inheritance. This does not mean that they were idle, but it did allow them an extensive social life of visits and entertainment. Lancaster could not offer the full range of pleasures to such people, and gentry society often gravitated to London, Bath or some regional centre such as York for at least part of the year. What social life Lancaster did have was concentrated into the period of the Assizes, the three fairs and the summer race meetings.

As the century wore on hours grew later in polite society. Dinner, which had begun the eighteenth century at about midday, had moved to 4 or 5 o'clock by the end, while dances and balls could often involve supper at 2 o'clock in the morning. While the gentry themselves could sleep it off the following day, there were a host of those that served them who had to keep the same hours. Coachmen, cooks, maidservants, waiters, musicians, sedan chair men, and link boys who carried torches to light the revellers home had to dance, as it were, to the same music, but without the pleasure.

The small group that constituted fashionable society in a town like Lancaster met regularly and was very familiar. Families would visit each other's houses in rotation, while larger parties required the use of the Assembly Rooms, where the building was designed so that two groups could meet at the same time without clashing. Tea-drinking, match-making, card-playing and marital intrigue would all go on to the background of local gossip.

The theatre was popular and performances would last several hours at a time, generally much longer than we are accustomed to, including perhaps

Lancaster's one surviving link extinguisher is seen here attached to the wall of number 76 Church Street, behind railings. This conical metal cap was probably originally part of a more prominent structure attached to the railings, such as those still to be seen in the New Town of Edinburgh. Here the link-boy would put out his flaming torch or flambeau after guiding the family back through the dark.

A rather ramshackle weather-boarded structure which formed the theatre or concert room in the back yard of the Horse & Farrier Inn in Church St in the 1770s. It was replaced by the purpose-built subscription theatre in St Leonardgate in 1781, now the Grand Theatre.

Lancaster City Museums

　　　LIFE IN GEORGIAN LANCASTER

Handbill for an evening's entertainment at the theatre in 1772. The mixed programme would have lasted some four hours, with *The Beggars' Opera* as the main feature. The travelling company of Heatton & Austin had a number of posters printed to which the dates could be added in ink later. In 1772 there was no permanent theatre in Lancaster and this programme was played in the strange little outbuilding in the yard of the Horse & Farrier Inn in Church Street. Just how an assembled cast of around twenty performers managed to stage a successful performance to a genteel audience in such a small building is quite beyond imagination.

Lancaster City Museums

left The new theatre in St Leonardgate, built in 1781 and financed by subscription. It had no permanent company, in common with most provincial theatres, and was used by travelling companies who put on a series of plays and entertainments from their repertoire, learning new plays as they walked between theatres on their circuit. Plays were put on during the Assizes and Race Week. This photograph shows it around 1900 when it was the Athenaeum.

By Meſſ. HEATTON and AUSTIN's Company.

At the new Theatre in the Horse and Farrier's Yard in LANCASTER;

On Monday being the 20 of July 1772, Will be perform'd The

BEGGARS OPERA.

Captin Mackheath, M. CUBIT, Peachum, Mr. EDWIN, Lockit, Mr. SMITH, Mat o'th' Mint, Mr. DUNCAN, Filch, Mr. JEFFRYS, Ben Budge, Mr. SIDDONS, Ninming Ned, Mr. BOGLE, Harry Paddington, Mr. HOOLE, Bob Booty, Mr. BIRCH, Jailor, Mr. EMERSON, Drawer, Mr. PEARSON, Harry Handy, Mr. PRESTON.
Polly, Mrs. BOGLE, Lucy and Mrs. Slammackin, Mrs. AUSTIN, Molly Brazen, Miſs PATTISON, Jenny Diver, Miſs HURST, Mrs. Coaxer, Mrs. DUNCAN, Sukey Tawdry, Mrs. JEFFRYS, Dolly Trull, Mrs. PEARSON, Mrs. Peachum and Diana Trapes, Mr. HEATTON.

End of the Play a new *Pantomime Interlude*, call'd The

WHIM:
OR,
HARLEQUIN's VAGARIES.

Harlequin, Mr. SIDDONS, & Pantaloon, Mr. SMITH, Clown, Mr. PRESTON. & Columbine, Mrs. JEFFRYS.

To which will be added a Farce, call'd The

APPRENTICE.

Dick, Mr. CUBIT, Wingate, Mr. EDWIN, Gargle, Mr. SMITH, Irish man, Mr. DUNCAN, Scotch-man, Mr. PEARSON, Preſident, Mr. BOGLE, First Spouter, Mr. SIDDONS, Watchman, BIRCH, Bailiff, Mr. PRESTON, Simon, Mr. JEFFRYS, Charlotte, Miſs HURST.

TICKETS to be had at the King's Arms, the Sun, and of Mr. HEATTON at his Lodgings.
The Days of Playing are Mondays, Wednesdays, and Fridays, and in the Race Week every Night.
To begin exactly at half an Hour paſt ſix o'Clock.

two plays and an 'entertainment'. For most of the eighteenth century the theatre outside London occupied a sort of no-man's-land on the edge of the law. Actors were considered to be little better than vagabonds. Initially Lancaster people went to see travelling players perform in Bulk tithe barn, just across the Jelle Beck and outside the borough boundary, where they were also beyond the borough's control. By the 1770s they used a strange little building in the yard of the Horse and Farrier Inn in Church Street as a theatre but in 1781 a new theatre (now the Grand Theatre) was purpose built by subscription in St Leonardgate. Eight subscribers of £50 each received 5 per cent from the rent and had a silver ticket giving the bearer free admission.[96] This represented thespian legitimacy at last. The new theatre was run by proprietors as one of a circuit. According to Christopher Clark in 1807 it had been run successively by Messrs Austin & Whitlock, Whitlock & Munden, Stephen Kemble, and Stanton in the twenty-five years or so of its existence.[97] The players travelled from theatre to theatre within the circuit, performing a large and changing repertoire of plays and roles, learning their lines as they rode or walked.[98] This theatre seems originally to have been called 'The Playhouse' but for a brief while in the early nineteenth century took the name of 'Theatre Royal'. Rev. W. MacRitchie went to see a performance in 1795:[99]

By Mr. MASON's Company of Comedians.

At the Theatre in the Meeting-House Lane,
On Wednesday Evening, July 21st, 1773

Will be presented the Celebrated COMEDY call'd

TUNBRIDGE WALKS;

OR,

The Yeoman of Kent.

Reynard, Mr. S L A N E Y.
Woodcock, Mr. B U C K,
Loveworth, Mr. W. M A S O N,
Maiden, Mr. M A S O N,
Squib, Mr. S T A N D E N.

Hillaria, Mrs. M A S O N,
Belinda, Miss B A R K E R,
Mrs. Goodfellow, Mrs. P E N N Y,
Penelope, Mrs. S T A N D E N,
Lucy, Mrs. M I L L S.

DANCING by Mr. FREEMAN.

To which will be added an English BURLETTA, call'd

The P A D L O C K.

Don Diego, Mr. W. M A S O N,
Leander, Mr. S L A N E Y,
Mungo (the Black Servant) Mr. M A S O N.

Leonora, Mrs. M A S O N,
Ursula, Mrs. M I L L S.

TICKETS to be had at Mr. Ashburner's Shop, the King's Arms, the Sun, and the New Inn.

PIT 2s. GAL. 1s.

To begin immediately after the Races.

... After dinner go to the Play. Mrs. Siddons in the character of Lady Macbeth; her brother Kemble plays Macbeth. The representation very tolerable on the whole, though Mrs. Siddons be poorly supported. Mrs. Siddons Benefit. A brilliant audience; the Lancashire ladies in all their charms ...

The tedium of daily life in a small town was sometimes broken by travelling curiosities, fairs and peepshows. In October 1802 the 'Irish Giant' O'Brien, who was nine feet tall (2.74 metres) could be seen for a shilling apiece at the Bull's Head in Cheapside. It was said that his party piece on walks for evening exercise was to frighten the Watch by lighting his pipe from the street lamps.[100]

In 1756 a certain William Hall was prosecuted in the Borough Courts for 'suffering a Bare to run loose in the publick streets of this borough the same being a public nuisance'. Presumably this was, when it behaved, a dancing bear. We should certainly know nothing of it were it not for Hall's court appearance.[101] Other entertainment of a less intellectual nature is hinted at by the visit to the Theatre in 1819 of Mr Usher, the celebrated clown, with his performing tom-cats and in the same year to the Assembly Room of Madame Ingleby, 'the South American fire-proof lady'.[102] In 1828 Madame Tussaud's wax-works paid Lancaster a visit, and were exhibited in the Assembly Room.[103]

In 1804 and 1808 the Circus came to town. On the first occasion[104] the New Circus parked on Green Ayre and put on performances both there and at the Theatre. It featured 'many surprising feats of horsemanship by a capital troop of equestrians', tightrope dancing and 'antipodean exercises' by Mr Cooke and Master Cimex (aged 8). The 1808 visit was by the New Olympic Circus[105] when Mr. Southby, the proprietor, was effusive about the 'liberal patronage already given' and 'overflowing houses'. The Circus, based in Cable Street, also gave benefit performances on the New Racecourse to help raise funds for the completion of the course, which was a shrewd attempt to win local support. The story does not, however, have a happy ending. The Circus was prosecuted in the borough court by a number of what seem to be financial creditors, including the splendidly named Moses Aaron James Gurney, licensee of the Cross Keys in Market Street. The court Rule Book gives a complete description of the Circus, surely a most unusual piece of evidence.

A wood erection, Circus, shed, or building situate on the Green Area in Lancaster with the boards, poles, springers, props, j[o]ists, spars, gallery and supporters, consisting of wood thereunto belonging with the iron cramps and nails therein, a quantity of boards round the ring or circle in the inside of the same circus, 5 poles, 2 pair of triangles, 1 spring board, 8 lamps, hoop with tin candlesticks, 6 blocks and ropes, 1 table, 4 wood candlesticks, several old boards, boxes and pieces of wood, 2 step ladders, 12 bass mats, a dressing room consisting of wood, a small wood shade, 7 wood supporters, a wood porch with several other articles of wood ...

All the boards, planks, supporters and timber with all the materials and fixtures ... forming ... the Circus on the Green Area.

Quantity of green baize, 1 cart and a pair of wheels.[106]

Subsequently it was sold for its materials.[107]

This was not the end of circuses for Lancaster. In November 1821 a visiting Circus in the Fryerage was blown to pieces by a violent storm.[108] Doubtless

there were many others of which we hear nothing, because no disaster over-
took them.

In 1785 Vincenzo Lunardi and his hydrogen balloon came to Lancaster
during race week at the behest of Richard Gillow for an ascent from the Castle
yard. While this does not seem to have actually taken place as planned (the
Gillow archive refers to cancellation notices) it may have gone ahead in the
following year.[109] No pictures survive from these attempts but a close parallel
can be drawn with J. C. Ibbetson's painting of George Biggin's ascent in
Lunardi's balloon from St George's Fields, London, on 29 June 1785.[110] A
balloon attempt of 1832 by a Mr Green, from the Gasworks at St George's
Quay (the balloon was filled with coal gas), was captured in a contemporary
pencil sketch.

Excessive drinking, common in the early eighteenth century, was giving way
by the 1760s and 1770s to more civilised behaviour, under the influence of
French manners. By modern standards, however, drinking was still on a huge
scale. Partly this was to do with the way in which many households brewed
their own beer. Small beer, from a second or third use of the mash, low in
alcohol, was used where we would drink tea, coffee, or fruit juices. Heavy
drinking was common at all levels of society and reached a peak at cele-
brations, races and fairs. At the festivities on the coming-of-age of Thomas

Pencil sketch showing
the intrepid Mr Green
and passengers taking
off in a balloon from St
George's Quay in 1832.
The location was
chosen because the Gas
Works were there, and
the balloon needed to
be filled with the highly
dangerous coal-gas.
Such events attracted
enormous crowds.

Lancaster City Museums

Butler Cole of Kirkland Hall in 1816 two of his tenants or workpeople died from excessive drinking (one indirectly by drowning while drunk).[111] This was regarded, in the manner of the times, as a tribute to the generosity of the entertainment.

As the eighteenth century wore on first coffee and then tea began to replace ale as the everyday drink, despite being extremely heavily taxed and very expensive. Tea-drinking remained an essentially feminine habit, and provided an opportunity to show off new china, the family silver and fashionable clothes. It was associated with a ritual of visiting among those with leisure, essentially the middle classes. On the evidence of the Rule Book, tea and coffee drinking were very widespread in Lancaster in the late Georgian period, but from the many references to brewing vessels home brewed ale was still very popular.

Dinner-parties provided an even bigger opportunity; display of exotic fruits, such as peaches or pineapples, helped to underline status. Gifts of cheeses, hot-house fruits, large joints of meat or poultry by country neighbours or from local estates could be the excuse for inviting friends in to dinner. Mahogany furniture by Gillow and others reflected the trend for entertaining, with extending tables, buffets to serve from and light elegant chairs. Gillows patented a telescopic table in 1800 which folded down to act as a small side table but extended with leaves when required. Newly rich families who had made their money from trade wanted a short-cut to elegance and would take advice from their suppliers on how their new furniture should be set out, so Gillows also produced large plans of room settings, a large number of which have survived. Houses were laid out for entertaining with suites of rooms linked together.

Gillows of Lancaster

The Gillow family of Lancaster are famous for their mahogany furniture, and early pieces now fetch considerable sums. It must be said that their contribution to English furniture-making had been largely forgotten until a revival of interest in the 1960s. Unlike most other makers, they frequently marked their work in characteristic places such as on the top of a drawer or on the leg of a chair. A very substantial archive helps to identify work, customers and personnel.

The Gillow dynasty was established by Robert Gillow, a poor Catholic orphan from Singleton in the Fylde, who was apprenticed to John Robinson

Fines of new Burgesses this year

Henry Marshall	1 : 0 : 0
Henry Wilson	1 : 0 : 0

Fines of new Burgesses this year

Henry Marshall	1 : 0 : 0
Henry Wilson	1 : 0 : 0
Henry Hole	1 : 6 : 8
John Crosfell	1 : 6 : 8
Robert Bell jun	1 : 0 : 0
George Haresnape	1 : 6 : 8
Robert Gillow	1 : 6 : 8
John Hale	1 : 6 : 8

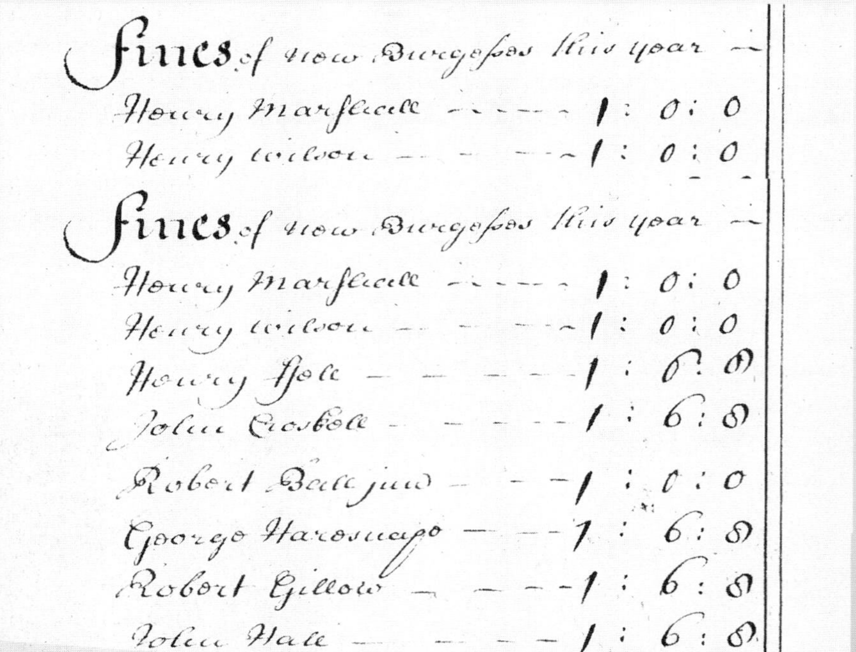

left Detail from Fines of New Burgesses, 1728, in the Bailiffs' accounts, showing the names of Robert Gillow and George Haresnape, who soon afterwards set up in trade together. Here they are just emerging from their seven-year apprenticeship. Gillow was the founder of the famous firm which bore his name.

29° July 1723°. Robtus Gillow fil Alicis Gillow de Great Singleton in Com Lanc
(153°)
...
27° Martij 1724. John Robinson

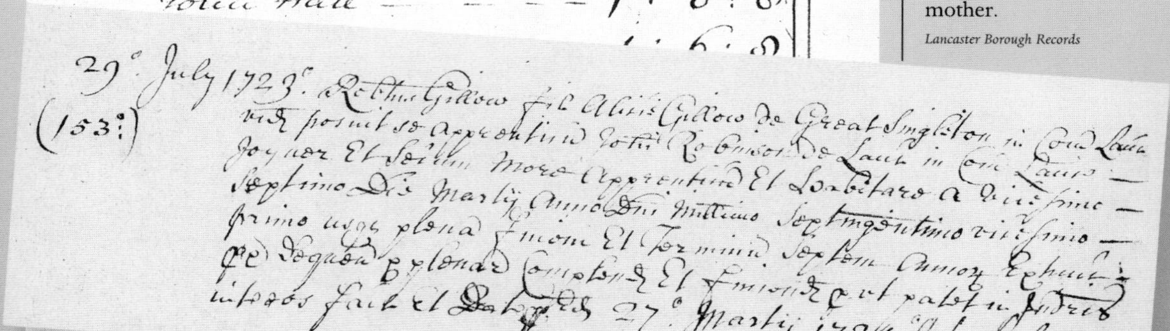

below Record of Robert Gillow's apprenticeship in 1721 in the Borough Apprentice Rolls. Such a record had to be made if the apprentice wanted to become a Freeman after seven years. Robert was the son of a poor Catholic widow from Singleton in the Fylde. Finding the money to have him apprenticed and losing his company for seven years must have been very difficult for his mother.

Lancaster Borough Records

of Lancaster in 1721. When he came out of his apprenticeship he set up in partnership with a fellow ex-apprentice, George Haresnape. He married in 1730 and in due course his two sons, Richard and Robert, joined him. Richard was trained as an architect in London, but joined the family business where his skills probably helped in the interior decoration side. In the year that Robert retired (1769) the firm opened a London branch in Oxford Street, which led to a great deal of business from fashionable society. The family prospered and in about 1830, by the third generation (Richard's son, another Richard) they had got out of trade and had become country gentlemen.

The business had its workshops on the Green Ayre, and offices on Castle Hill. It had a reputation for fine workmanship. Lancaster was at this date a sub-regional centre for furniture, quite apart from Gillows' London connection. Fine timber came through the port – principally mahogany, but with numerous other types used for banding and inlay. The firm outlived its family connections and in the early twentieth century joined with the Liverpool firm of Waring to become Waring & Gillow, later still a high street name which survived several changes of ownership and a decline in quality. The Lancaster manufacturing connection was broken with the closure of the works in 1962. Good examples of Gillow furniture may be seen in the City Museum, the Judges Lodging Museum, and Leighton Hall, the family home.

Tombstone recording burials of members of the Gillow family, who were Catholics. Richard Gillow, the son of Robert, founder of the firm of Gillow, was trained in London as an architect, and designed several Lancaster buildings including the Custom House. However, so successful was the firm in the field of cabinet-making that he had little time to devote to architecture.

Gillow & Co.'s Castle Hill offices.

Church Life CHAPTER TEN

Lancaster's parish church (the Priory church) dominated the local Georgian religious scene. Although life for Catholics and nonconformists became gradually easier as the eighteenth century progressed, the Church of England was the established church, and the church did far more than administer religious affairs. A great deal of non-religious local administration was carried out through its network: the diocese of York, the Archdeaconry of Richmond, and individual parish vestry meetings. There was no equivalent civil network such as government, region, county council, district council, parish council, as there is today. The church had tentacles everywhere. Until 1836 – theoretically – landowners and farmers still had to paid tithes (a tenth of all produce growing in or on the soil) in kind to their rector. In practice many rectors had long ago settled for a 'composition' (money payment) in lieu. Lancaster parish even had its own Act of Parliament for Corn Rents in 1824, which in practice was much like the later widespread Tithe Awards.[112] The vestry controlled the local poor law, while the diocese kept all records of baptisms, marriages and burials, and wills were proved in the Archdeaconry courts. Church courts could still punish certain sorts of wrongdoing, and this could involve the perpetrator doing penance while dressed in a white sheet during the church service. This happened in Lancaster as late as 1824. Anglicans dominated society even in this strongly Catholic area, and the influence of the Anglican church was all-pervading. Non-Anglicans had a built-in disadvantage.

Despite this overwhelming power, the Anglican church at this period was run with extraordinary laxity. It is hard for us to comprehend the attitude towards the rich pickings of the church, involving absentee and multiply-beneficed clergymen, not to mention the higher clergy, coming as we do from the other side of the Victorian reforms. It would probably be the lack of enthusiasm (regarded as rather dangerous and un-English!) and the degree of laissez-faire which would strike us most if we could go back.

At the beginning of the eighteenth century Lancaster was a typical huge northern parish, encompassing parts of the Lune valley and even detached portions on the outskirts of Preston and Liverpool. Essentially it was still as it had been in the Middle Ages. The forces of conservatism in the church were bolstered by an unwillingness to share the revenues among a number of smaller parishes, although this would have been sensible from many points of view. There was still only one parish church. Everyone within the parish had to come to Lancaster at least to be christened, married or buried, apart from those who lived within chapelries with local rights. The civil governance of this parish was by the Vicar and 'the Twenty-four' or 'the 24tie' (four-and-twenty) who represented its various townships and who included the Mayor of the borough in their number.[113]

By the 1750s the population had grown and a new church, St John's, was built on the Green Ayre to serve the people living there. It was joined in 1796 by St Anne's, which served the more evangelical members of the Anglican church, known then as 'enthusiasts', under Rev. Housman.

All of these churches were adapted, or, in the case of the last two, designed, for preaching, which had become the main function of Anglican ritual in the Georgian period. Church and theatre had come close in their desire to provide the maximum seating with the best view of the pulpit or stage. This congruence certainly aided the later conversion of St Anne's into the Duke's Theatre.

St John's church, built on the Green Ayre in the 1750s to supplement the priory church. The tower was added some thirty years later.

The priory church was filled with four rows of box pews and a prominent pew known as 'Noah's Ark' which occupied the centre of the aisle right below the pulpit. Not surprisingly it became a bone of contention and was removed in 1825.[114] The pews ran right through the chancel arch, hemming in the altar and ignoring the ancient architectural and liturgical division between nave and chancel. Galleries carried another tier of seating above them, and a very large congregation could be, and was, housed. Across the east end were placed the ornately carved medieval choir stalls, cutting off an area to serve as Diocesan Registry and as a vestry, until a new extension was added to the north in the late 1820s, providing space for these functions.[115] Pews in all the churches were regarded as private property and were decorated and furnished in individualistic style and could be left by will, rented or sold.

The priory church may once have had a band of musicians, and certainly had a 'singers' pew' for a West Gallery choir in 1724 but the very early introduction of an organ in 1728 and with it more polite views on how church music should sound stifled the development of more popular traditions for the remainder of the century.[116] The very distinguished Langshaws, father and son, were organists here from 1772.

Handbill for seats in St John's Chapel. Pews were a commodity to be bought, sold or rented. Those in the best positions to see and hear the preacher commanded the highest prices, and many owners had their pews lined with green or red baize and fitted with cushions for comfort.

Lancaster Central Library

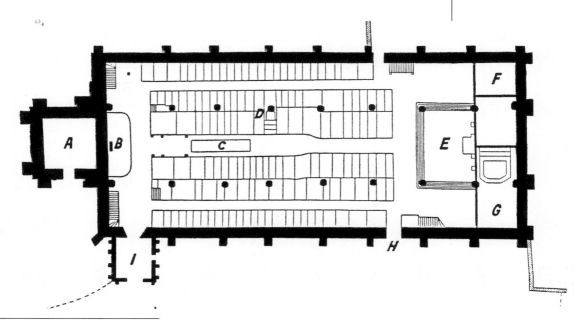

right Plan and partial sections through galleries of Lancaster Priory church. The precise date is unknown, but must be after 1825 when the large and obtrusive pew known as 'Noah's Ark' was removed. Despite the building of other churches such as St John's and St Anne's during the eighteenth century the Priory church was still required to house an enormous congregation at the main festivals.

Binns' Collection, Liverpool

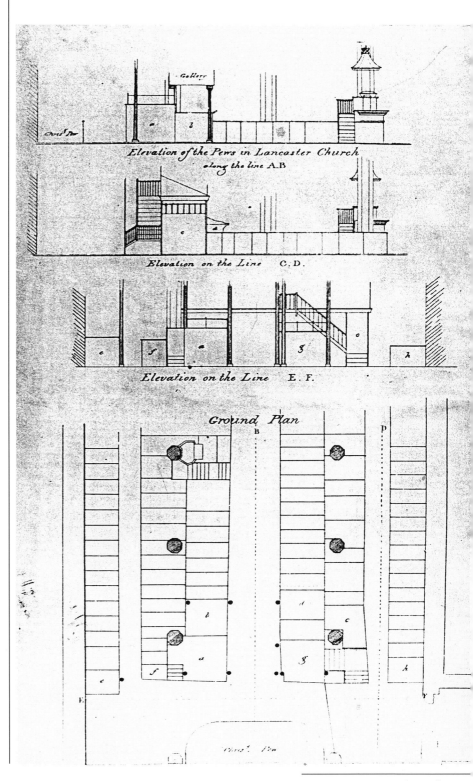

Elevation of the Pews in Lancaster Church along the line A.B.

Elevation on the Line C.D.

Elevation on the Line E.F.

Ground Plan

left Plan of Lancaster Priory church as it was in 1819. The east end was fenced off by the medieval choir stalls and contained the vestry and consistory court where wills were proved. The rest of the church was filled with pews and galleries to accommodate as many people as possible within sight and sound of the pulpit. Below the pulpit was a great private pew known as 'Noah's Ark', removed six years after this plan was made.

Catholicism had survived several centuries in Lancashire by lying low in the face of persecution. It had long been dangerous to be a Catholic and Lancaster's Catholic population had worshipped in secret during penal times, while often outwardly conforming to the Church of England. Georgian Catholics had met slightly more openly in a converted barn in Mason Street, within Gillows' cabinet-making workshop area.[117] Events such as the Gordon Riots in London in 1780 showed how dangerous it could still be for them, but by the late 1790s tolerance had grown to the extent that congregations could worship in their own chapel without hindrance. The new Catholic chapel in Dalton Square was opened in 1798. It is now Palatine Hall, one of the City Council offices. (Its relatively short life as a chapel was due to the building of St Peter's, in East Road, now the Cathedral.) Despite the openness of worship, this chapel was designed to fit discreetly into the townscape and could well have been mistaken on its southern frontage for a gentleman's house. Catholics dominated certain trades in Lancaster such as cabinet-making, largely because of the success of the Catholic Gillow family, who recruited many of their co-religionists as apprentices. The Gillows also provided discreet funding for many Catholic activities, as did the Dalton family of Thurnham. Lord Fauconberg, one of the Bellasis family of Newburgh Priory, Yorkshire, who lived in Thurnham Street, was another pillar of the local Catholic community and one of the few members of the gentry to live in the town.

Although nonconformists had also had a difficult time in the seventeenth century their fortunes had started to rise by the Georgian period, despite still being barred from a number of official activities. Quakers would not swear the oath of allegiance to the Crown – or any oath for that matter – so could not take any office or even become Freemen, unless a friendly authority allowed them to 'affirm' instead, thus avoiding an oath. Pushed by their circumstances into trade, they did extraordinarily well, at least in part because their trustworthiness was generally taken for granted. Their meeting-house was first built in 1677 but was rebuilt and extended in 1708 and 1779. It consisted of several spaces including the meeting-house proper, containing benches facing in towards the centre, one of which, known as a 'stand', was for the elders. Above one end, and originally with communicating shutters to open or close at will, was the Women's meeting-house. There was also a school and the whole complex was used for many social and non-religious purposes, since the Friends provided an almost complete social framework for members. The meeting-house also provided a venue for regular Yearly Meetings for Friends from the northern area.[118] The Quaker Rawlinson family had powerful interests in trade and manufacturing of all sorts and built a series of dynastic connections with other families of the Quaker merchant elite.[119]

Congregationalists (Independents) and Unitarians (Presbyterians) had also

Lancaster's Quaker Meeting House was built outside the town beside a road into the western fields later known as Meeting House Lane. From persecuted minority in the seventeenth century Quakers rapidly became the backbone of the business community, and their growth was marked by successive extensions of the Meeting House during the eighteenth century.

laboured under difficulties in earlier times but by the eighteenth century had joined the main stream of toleration. They had their own chapels in High Street, built 1772, and in St Nicholas Street, rebuilt 1786. Methodists were a relatively late arrival, using a couple of cottages in Damside Street for their chapel; their first purpose-built chapel, in Sulyard Street, was not put up until 1805. For most non-Anglicans their faith or sect was tremendously important socially, setting them apart, and providing a complete social and marital network. Politics came into it as well: Anglicanism and Toryism were closely related, as were Non-Conformism and Whiggery. Catholics and Quakers married among their own kind and suffered ostracism from their community if they 'married out', while Non-Conformist merchants favoured each other with business. There is no doubt that Georgian Lancaster, with substantial minorities of all these kinds, had a series of interlocking but separate social circles within its relatively small population. Despite this variety the small size of the population meant that most of the time people had to get along with each other and overt religious differences were rare.

Postscript

Lancaster enjoyed a period of prosperity and good taste during the second half of the eighteenth century. This was reflected in new buildings, new institutions, and a sense of pride and confidence in the town. At the end of the century things went wrong for Lancaster. The war with Revolutionary France took a high toll of local shipping. Average ship size was growing and becoming too great for the river Lune to accommodate. Facilities such as marine insurance concentrated in ports like Liverpool. The West Indies began to lose their economic advantage. The two Lancaster banks, Worswick's and Dilworth's, collapsed in the 1820s within a few years of each other, taking with them over £400,000 in local savings. The failure was compounded by the fact that many who had just recovered part of their deposit from the first collapse had reinvested it in the latter bank.[120]

Whatever the cause the effects were quite clear. Building, unless it was funded by outside bodies, came to a sudden halt. Many merchants went bankrupt, while some of those that did not moved their base of operations to Liverpool, which continued to grow. Textile mills, which had until now made little impression on the town, now began to occupy the level ground alongside the canal, utilising cheap coal brought by canal and cheap labour now available within Lancaster. For the next century and a half Lancaster became a working-class textile town, little different in certain respects from those of East Lancashire.

The grand Georgian buildings were sub-divided and treated with disrespect, but at least they survived. There was not enough money around to knock down these relics from the high water mark of Lancaster's prosperity. But in the 1970s realisation began to dawn that they formed one of Lancaster's greatest assets, and could help to set the future tone of the town, especially areas such as St George's Quay. Serious efforts began to put them back into order and protect them from the more unsympathetic uses and alterations.

More recently we have begun to understand how people lived and used these buildings in what must have been a high point in the economic and cultural life of the town. We can also look back, without too much help from rose-tinted spectacles, to see a smaller, more compact and uncrowded town enjoying a high standard of living for most of its citizens, surrounded at an easy distance by beautiful countryside and possessing many objects of elegance and beauty.

Notes

1 K. H. Docton, 'Lancaster 1684', *Historic Society of Lancashire & Cheshire*, 109 (1957), pp. 125–42.

2 C. Clark, *An Historical and Descriptive Account of the Town of Lancaster*, 2nd edn (1811), pp. 119–20.

3 J. West, *Town Records* (1983), pp. 320–1.

4 A. White, *The Buildings of Georgian Lancaster*, 2nd edn (2000).

5 J. D. Marshall, *The Autobiography of William Stout of Lancaster 1665–1752* (1967), pp. 236–7.

6 F. McLynn, *The Jacobite Army in England 1745: the Final Campaign* (1998), esp. pp. 68–76, 158–60, 168–70.

7 I. G. Brown and H. Cheape, *Witness to Rebellion: John Maclean's Journal of the 'Forty-Five and the Penicuik Drawings* (1996), p. 26.

8 A. J. Noble and J. S. Hayes, *The 1757 Militia Ballot List for South Lonsdale (Lancashire)* (1997).

9 Lancaster Borough Records; Rule Book 1784–1822, ff. 118–20

10 E. Hall (ed.), *Miss Weeton, Journal of a Governess*, vol. 1 (1807–11, 1936), pp. 6–8.

11 W. O. Roper, *Materials for the History of the Church of Lancaster*, IV, Chetham Society, 59 (1906), p. 695.

12 Rotherham Central Library 2/FI/1.

13 E. C. Freeston, *Prisoner of War Ship Models 1775–1825* (1973).

14 C. Chalklin, *English Counties and Public Building 1650–1830* (1998).

15 Lancaster Borough Records, Book Kb, Orders of Council & Elections 1794–1822, f. 248; P. Williamson, *From Confinement to Community: The Moving Story of 'The Moor', Lancaster's County Lunatic Asylum* (n.d., but 1999).

16 Marshall, *Stout Autobiography*, pp. 102, 205.

17 M. Elder, *The Slave Trade and the Economic Development of Eighteenth-century Lancaster* (1992), pp. 195–7

18 W. Cowan (ed.), *A Journey to Edenborough in Scotland by Joseph Taylor, Late of the Inner Temple, Esq. (1705)* (1903), p. 161.

19 HMC Portland, VI, 190

20 B. G. Hutton, 'A Lakeland journey, 1759', *Cumberland & Westmorland Antiquarian & Archaeological Society*, 2nd ser., LXI (1961), p. 290.

21 Monson, Lincolnshire Archives Office, Monson 15/B/2 ff. 12–14.

22 C. P. Fendall and E. A. Crutchley, *The Diary of Benjamin Newton Rector of Wath 1816–1818* (1933), pp. 203–4.

23 Lancaster Central Library, Obituaries Scrapbook, obituary of Canon Grenside, 1916.

24 R. Bond, 'Some events of seventy years', *Lancaster Philosophical Society Transactions* (1891), pp. 81–2.

25 T. Gray, quoted in T. West, *A Guide to the Lakes in Cumberland, Westmorland, and Lancashire*, 3rd edn (1784), p. 214.

26 W. Wordsworth, *Guide to the Lakes* (1835), p. 8.

27 Anon, Nottinghamshire Record Office, M380.

28 L. Noble, Yorkshire Archaeological Society YAS: DD70/142.

29 T. Gray in West, *Guide to the Lakes*, 216; Clark, *Historical and Descriptive Account*, pp. 114–16, quoting the *Annual Register*, 1760.

30 Monson, Lincolnshire Archives Office.

31 T. Mowl, *To Build the Second City: Architects and Craftsmen of Georgian Bristol* (1991), *passim*.

32 Lancaster City Museums, acc. no. LM67.73.

33 *Lancaster 50 years ago July 1850–Dec. 1851* (1902), p. 249.

34 Bill in Lancaster City Museums, acc. no. LM2000.38/1.

35 Anon (Simond, Louis), *Journal of a Tour and Residence in Great Britain During the years 1810 and 1811 by a French Traveller* (2 vols), New York (1815), p. 256.

36 Dr. S. H. Spiker, Librarian to the King of Prussia, *Travels through England, Wales, and Scotland* (1816, 1820), pp. 282–8.

37 S. Bamford, *Passages in the Life of a Radical* (c.1819) (1984), pp. 196–214.

38 Bond, 'Some events of seventy years', pp. 80–1.

39 A. Hewitson, *Northward Between Preston and Lancaster* (1900), p. 44.

40 *Lancaster Gazette*, 15 Jan. 1827 and 10 March 1827.

41 *Lancaster Gazette*, 10 March 1827.

42 A. Murray (ed.), *A Biographical Register of the Royal Grammar School Lancaster*, nd, pp. 9–47.

43 Baines' *Directory*, 1825.

44 Rule Book 1784–1822, ff. 32–3.

45 Lancaster Central Library, MS 3706.

46 A. Fraser, *A Verbatim Report of the Cause Doe Dem. Tatham v Wright, tried at the Lancaster Lammas Assizes*, vol. 1 (1834), pp. 348–59.

47 Deeds, in private possession.

48 Noble and Hayes, op. cit.

49 Lancaster City Council, Deeds 198/2; deeds in private possession.

50 *Post-Medieval Archaeology Newsletter*, Summer 2000.

51 A. J. White, 'Lancaster and the West Indies', *Contrebis*, 9 (1981), pp. 21–2.

52 Family papers lent by Simon Barrow and transcribed by Nigel Dalziel: copy in Lancaster Maritime Museum. E. Kennerley, *The Brockbanks of Lancaster: The Story of an Eighteenth-century Shipbuilding Firm*, Lancaster Museum Monograph (1981), p. 16.

53 Marshall, *Autobiography of William Stout*.

54 Lancaster Borough Records, Rule Book, 1784–1822.

55 Clark, op. cit., 56.

56 Lancaster Borough Records, Book G; Lancaster Central Library, Apprentice Rolls, MSS 158,160.

57 Lancaster City Council, Deeds 2457.

58 Carmen's Rules, 1830. Lancaster City Museums LM89.69.

59 Rule Book, 1784–1822, f. 117.

60 Ibid, f. 126.

61 Ibid, f. 73.

62 Clark, op. cit., 51.

63 Lancaster City Museums, acc. no. LM82.9; J. Press, 'The Collapse of a

Contributory Pension Scheme: the Merchant Seamen's Fund, 1747–1851', *Journal of Transport History*, 5, 2 (1979), pp. 91–104.

64 *Lancaster Gazette*, 28 Feb. 1811; the cup is currently on loan to the National Maritime Museum.

65 Copy of will in deeds of 12 Castle Park.

66 *The Lonsdale Magazine*, 1 (1820), p. 469.

67 Lancaster Central Library, Scrapbook 5 pt 2, f. 66.

68 White, *Buildings of Georgian Lancaster*.

69 Ibid., pp. 3, 50–1.

70 *The Lonsdale Magazine*, 1 (1820), pp. 421–2.

71 M. Girouard, *The English Town* (1990), pp. 145–54.

72 D. Foskett, *John Harden of Brathay Hall, 1772–1847* (1974), p. 6.

73 Rule Book 1784–1822, f. 165.

74 Lancaster Central Library, Sessions Book 1737–66, MS102, 1740, f. 21.

75 For example, Lancaster Borough Records; Book H Bailiffs Accounts 1772–96, f. 4 (1772); f. 258 (1787).

76 Lancaster Borough Records; Book Kb 1794–1822 Orders of Council & Elections, f. 47 (1797).

77 *Lancaster Gazette*, 22 Jan. 1803.

78 Lancaster Central Library, Scrapbook 2.3

79 *Lancaster Gazette*, 19 Sept. 1812.

80 M. Winstanley in A. White (ed,), *A History of Lancaster*, 2nd edn (2001), p. 208.

81 *Lancaster Gazette*, 24 Feb. 1827.

82 Lancaster Central Library, Scrapbook 2.4 (n.d. but *c.* 1810).

83 *The Lonsdale Magazine*, 1 (1820), p. 472.

84 Lancaster Central Library, Sessions Book 1802–35, MS 3333, 14 Oct. 1802.

85 Ibid.

86 *Lancaster Gazette*, 16 July 1811; 28 Oct. 1824.

87 *Lancaster Gazette*, 15 Jan. 1829.

88 Lancaster Central Library, Sessions Book 1737–1766, MS102, ff. 100, 165.

89 Lancaster Borough Records, Rentals for the fee farm rent in Bailiffs' Accounts, Book F, 1736–71, *passim*.

90 *English Dialect Dictionary*.

91 Lancaster Borough Records, Minute Book, 1756–94.

92 Lancaster Borough Records, Rule Book, 1784–1822, ff. 8, 71.

93 Ibid, f. 80.

94 Ibid, f. 88.

95 White, *Buildings of Georgian Lancaster*, pp. 21–2, 45.

96 *The Lonsdale Magazine*, 1 (1820), p. 470.

97 Clark, *Historical & Descriptive Account*, 45.

98 A. Betjeman, *The Grand Theatre, Lancaster: Two Centuries of Entertainment* (1982); S. Rosenfeld, *The Georgian Theatre of Richmond, Yorkshire, and its circuit* (1984).

99 Rev. W. MacRitchie, *Diary of a Tour through Great Britain in 1795* (1897), pp. 35–6.

100 *Lancaster Gazette*, 8 Oct. 1802.

101 Lancaster Central Library, Sessions Book 1737–66, MS102, f99

102 *Lancaster Gazette*, 3 May 1819.

103 *Lancaster Gazette*, 11 Oct. 1828.

104 *Lancaster Gazette*, 5 May 1804.

105 *Lancaster Gazette*, 19 March 1808.

106 Rule Book 1784–1822, f. 96ff.

107 *Lancaster Gazette*, 2 July 1808.

108 *Lancaster Gazette*, 30 Nov. 1821.

109 S. E. Stuart and W. T. W. Potts, 'Richard Gillow and Vincent Lunardi: Early Balloon Flights and the Lancaster Balloon Mystery', *Contrebis*, XXIV (1999), pp. 26–33.

110 Cf. J. Mitchell, *Julius Caesar Ibbetson 1759–1817* (1999), pp. 3, 61.

111 *Lancaster Gazette*, 11 Nov. 1816.

112 E. J. Evans, *Tithe Maps, Apportionments and the 1836 Act*, British Association for Local History (1993), p. 11.

113 W. O. Roper, *Materials for the History of the Church of Lancaster*, vol. 3, Chetham Soc. 58 (1906), *passim*.

114 Roper, op. cit., 649ff.

115 Roper, op. cit., *passim*; vol. 4, p. 686.

116 A. White, 'Church Bands and Singers in North Lancashire' (Lancaster University Centre for North-West Regional Studies), *Regional Bulletin*, 12 (1998), pp. 93–9.

117 Lancaster Central Library, Scrapbook 2 (folio) contains a description.

118 D. M. Butler, *Quaker Meeting Houses of Britain* (1999), 1, pp. 306–12.

119 A. Raistrick, *Quakers in Science and Industry* (1968).

120 A. White (ed.), *Beauties of the North: Lancaster in 1820* (1989), intro.; *Lancaster Gazette*, 13 Feb. 1822; 10 Feb. 1826.

Index

Pages marked in bold refer to captions to illustrations.